The Exponential Life

Joil A. Marbut

Library of Congress Control Number: 2024932412
ISBN-13: 979-8-9899531-0-3

Printed in the United States of America
1st edition 2024

Cover artwork and book design by Leah Ash M.
Fourth Seat Collective Publishing: fscpublishing.com

To my father.

The man who taught me what an exponential life looked like by simply living it out before me. You were a mystic and a contemplative, even if you never heard the words nor knew their definitions. Every day you sought silence and solitude, yet you loved the noise of family. You enjoyed watching the world come alive and being reborn with each morning's sunrise. You prayed and you listened to God's voice. You lived the liturgy of laughter. You loved without conditions. You reminded me to slow down and not to wish my life away. You cried with those who cried and you were the first to celebrate the victories of others.

Pops, "Till we meet at Jesus' feet."

"The Glory of God is the human
being fully alive."
- Irenaeus Early Church father

"The Pentecostal power, when you sum
it all up, is just more of God's love.
If it does not bring more love,
it is simply a counterfeit."
- William Seymour,
Early Pentecostal pioneer

Contents

Preface viii

Introduction xii

Outsetting to Exponential 2

1. Rumors of Something More 3

2. The Exponential Life 21

3. On-Ramps to the Exponential Life 42

Paradoxical Imperatives for Relating to God 63

4. On-Ramp of Listening 65

5. On-Ramp of Prayer 92

Paradoxical Imperatives for Relating to Others 117

6. On-Ramp of Wilderness 119

7. On-Ramp of Community 142

Paradoxical Imperatives for Relating to Self 167

8. On-Ramp of Self-Denial 169

9. On-Ramp of Sabbath 189

Paradoxical Imperatives for Relating to (Citizenship in) Heaven and Earth 207

10. On-Ramp of Generosity 209

11. On-Ramp of Beholding 228

Embracing Exponential 251

12. Our Ultimate Goal 253

Conclusion 272

Acknowledgments

This work has taken decades to write and a team to complete. To Chris Hall, you lit the fire that would become this book, and by giving it a few readings, each time you said, "It's a good book," you kept me going. To my father-in-law, Bill, thank you for proofing it and pushing me through to publication. To Nick Serban, your work and buy-in have made this possible. To Mitchell Capps, you, my friend, made this readable and added valuable questions to the text. John W Kennedy, you are the Jedi master of editors, thank you. To my mom for believing in me from the start and encouraging me to write. To the exponential pastors and church leaders of Morona Santiago, Ecuador, you have served as my laboratory; you have loved me through my successes and failures. To my children, Drew, Will, Emelia and Aidan, you have given me a lesson in our Heavenly Father's love for us. And finally to my anchor, she is my everything. Leah you put up with the process, you listened to ramblings that made no sense, you proofread, corrected, and added loving and thoughtful touches on this work and its layout. We are going to change the world.

Preface

THIS JOURNEY WAS BORN in a comment gently nestled inside the corner of a casual conversation. As a follower of Christ, I am firmly aware of my personal experience with God. I remember that well before I knew my Enneagram personality type or Myers-Briggs test results, I had a very firm grasp on my relationship with God. This understanding came in large part from digesting Richard Foster's life-changing book *Streams of Living Water*.

As a result of savoring this wonderful work, I realized that I had primarily existed and lived in the Charismatic stream. I, along with my Charismatic, Pentecostal, Full Gospel, Spirit-filled, Bapticostal, and other modern mystic friends live in a church world that is filled with the tangible reality of a God who does speak to us on a regular basis, whether through the written Word of God, a prophetic gift, tongues and interpretation, or even a still small voice. My spiritual habitat evolved with those whose life is filled with the ever-present expectation that he could be saying something right now.

The "word" that launched this book was spoken over lunch during a spiritual retreat week, between mouthfuls of roast beef and asparagus where Dr. Christopher A. Hall casually changed my outlook without even trying. Chris has been a spiritual director in my life, the president of Renovaré, professor, and author, yet at that moment he slid into the chair as my muse. I asked him several questions and listened to his fatherly response. I made my way through a list of things I'd been saving to pick his brain about: various points concerning my life, my family, and a book I was writing.

I never really got to the subject of the book. Chris continued to listen graciously as I struggled for words. Then in a charismatically supernatural — or at least a rather serendipitous moment — he smiled and said, "I hope it is a book about spiritual formation for Pentecostals. That is a book I would be interested to see." For a brief moment, it seemed to me that time and matter ceased. As I found myself joining the "burning heart club," I realized that not only was someone else interested in *that* book, but it was, in fact, *the* book that I was struggling so desperately to put into words.

His comment allowed me to see my unique position in the church world. Soon after my new birth into the kingdom of God, I found myself seeking what I had heard promised each week in the small Pentecostal church I attended. I had questions, inquiries, and curiosities about this experience laid out in the Book of Acts and sprinkled through Paul's epistles. That same power the disciples received in the Upper Room was apparently available to me. I found trustworthy guides in my own family who helped me wrestle with my doubts and reservations. As a result, I was ushered into the Charismatic stream at the kitchen table of my aunt and uncle's country home in my rural Alabama hometown. It was only the beginning.

This journey has led me to the caves and the monasteries of the desert, the brush harbors of the Great Awakenings, and the tents and storefronts of the early Pentecostal revivals. The path eventually brought me to the teachings of spiritual formation giants Richard Baxter, John Wesley, Dallas Willard, Henri Nouwen, Brennan Manning, the aforementioned Richard Foster, and others. They have served as guides to a deeper life. The further I journeyed with them, the richer and fuller my life became. This led me to understand that there was more, much more than what I was seeing week in and week out in my local church. It has provided the fodder of the central conversation that has been ongoing over the years of marriage I have shared with my fellow pilgrim wife, Leah. It has also served as the basis for my family's missionary work of church planting in the Amazon jungle in Ecuador. These vicarious relationships urged me to explore the other "streams" of experience. As I learned, I could tell I was only touching the tip of the proverbial iceberg and my hunger kept growing. I did not want to miss out on anything.

As I probed deeper, I realized not many of "us" (Pentecostal/Charismatics) were making the journey. As I reached out to others about my spiritual experience, I received mixed responses. Some were excited at the possibilities. Others were afraid of what it might mean for their lives or couldn't help but remember disreputable accounts they had heard from others in the same vein. I suddenly felt as though I could empathize with Joshua and Caleb upon returning from their reconnaissance mission to the Promised Land. I seized every opportunity to explain the amazing things that I had beheld to the hearts of the unseeing. I knew I had seen the beauty of the full gospel life as a result of spiritual formation, and I desperately wanted to draw a picture to serve as a map for seekers and skeptics alike.

This book is my attempt to draw that picture. In it, I hope you'll see for yourself what can transpire when a man or woman chooses to allow God to make them "fully alive." I pray it will serve as a map to the Land of Promise. It is a map born in a comment gently nestled inside the corner of a casual conversation. Thank you, Chris, for giving a "word in due season." You are deeply loved.

Introduction

IS THERE MORE than what we can see at the tips of our fingers? What if we are viewing things upside down, through tinted eyeglasses or in a skewed manner? What if our coming to faith and being baptized in water and being baptized in the Spirit is not the end but just the beginning? What if we have been staring at the spiritual stairwell and what we thought were the final steps, when in fact they were nothing more than the first two or three steps that lead us to an even deeper life? Is there something in you that yearns for more? Can you hear the Spirit calling you to "come further up and come further in?"[1]

Perhaps you have begun to feel the need to invert your understanding. Maybe you feel as though you've settled for too little. It's neither difficult nor uncommon to content

---

[1] Original Quote, "I have come home at last! This is my real country! I belong here. This is the land I have been look- ing for all my life, though I never knew it till now. The reason why we loved the old Narnia is that is sometimes looked a little like this. Bree-hee- hee! Come further up, come further in!." C.S. Lewis, *The Last Battle,* (HarperTrophy, 2000), 195-197.

oneself with your previous participation in water and Spirit baptism and then entertain no other plans except to simply hang on and hunker down until Jesus comes. This approach is far away from Jesus' proclamation of a "kingdom come," a kingdom that's said to be "at hand." Do those descriptors make you curious? These promised proclamations should, as they were intended, make you wonder what you are missing.

When asked in Luke 10 by a religious leader for his summary of the law, Jesus did not hesitate to answer. He replied to the inquiry this way: "Love the Lord your God with all your heart, soul, mind, and strength, and the second is like it, to love your neighbor as yourself."[2] This concise answer could not be any clearer. It requires no debate. Nothing is hidden or enigmatic about it. Jesus is straightforward and to the point. The center of our Christian universe is to learn to love God in all aspects of our lives. When he says "heart, soul, mind, and strength," he is describing the sum of human faculty, sense, and even the less tangible configurations of our innermost being.

Yet in the Charismatic stream of the Church, this holistic approach to loving God has been sidelined far too often by generations of believers. Instead, we seek shortcuts in an attempt to somehow magically "leapfrog" us into a driver's seat of supernatural authority, all while bypassing the

[2] NIV

commitment to become true lovers of our God. This has manifested itself in the volumes of books written to explain the formula for getting guaranteed answers for mostly self-serving prayers, or how to live a life of greater comfort and fewer inconveniences. Such texts are churned out again and again, with no mention of loving God more or truly becoming his disciple. Yet if we are to be obedient to Jesus' "Greatest Command," it will require that we love both God and our neighbor. To do this, we must be willing to allow ourselves to be stretched by the Holy Spirit.

As Charismatics, we know that the reality of Pentecost has given us a personal spiritual trainer who "leads us and guides us into all truth."[3] We are well acquainted with the wonderful Paraclete: our Helper who never leaves us. Yet in our unswerving commitment to "live in the Spirit," it can be easy to not see the forest for the trees. We want to be so "in tune" with the Holy Spirit that we overlook the clearest path to obedient fulfillment found in the command to love God deeply and our neighbor as ourselves.

In our Pentecostal passion, we risk missing Jesus. Just look at the example Jesus left us in the Incarnation. Can we ever truly take on his yoke if we are unwilling to walk the path he laid out? William Seymour, Pentecostal pioneer and father of the Azusa Street Revival, said, "There are many wells today, but they are dry. There are many hungry

---

[3] John 16:13

souls today that are empty. But let us come to Jesus and take Him at His Word and we will find wells — for Jesus is that well."[4] This book is an invitation to you to do just that, to simply take Jesus "at His Word" and, as a result, to allow yourself to be filled to your fullest capacity with Him.

My heart's desire has been to write a book that will point you to the paths that Jesus laid out during his time on earth. The same paths served his first disciples and are meant to serve his disciples today. These paths lead us to love God deeply and to the well that will never run dry. May it be spiritual nourishment to each pilgrim who picks it up. While I long to speak to a broad audience, this is not intended to be a milkshake book to pick up at the drive-through and sip on your way home. I hope that inside each chapter you will find meat that will help you grow and spiritual sustenance that needs to be savored, chewed, and digested.

---

[4] William Seymour, *The Great Azusa Street Revival: The Life and Sermons of William Seymour*, (Whitaker House, 2020), 75.

Outsetting to Exponential

1. Rumors of Something More

YOU COULD SAY that this book had its beginning about 300 miles from the table I shared with Chris that day just outside the back door of my childhood home. When I was 6 years old, the greatest adventure in the world was the wooded thicket at the back corner of the cow pasture that stood behind our house. I sneaked out every chance I got to climb in and around the trees and to search through the various rusting piles of broken farm equipment and old appliances that had been left by their previous owners.

But at the end of my expedition, I always found myself at the same place. I climbed to the top of the small hill just beyond the thicket and looked out on the remaining half mile to the greater forest that hugged the snaking river running through its heart. My parents had laid the limits for my explorations. Each time I would go to the very edge of those barriers and usually, as you might expect with a curious little boy, just a step or two beyond.

By nature I am an explorer. Over the years, this drive to see what I was missing out on has led me down many rivers, large and small. It has led me along numerous forgotten roads, into valley depths, and mountain heights. Every time I see a mountain that I have not yet explored, I find myself imagining the view from the summit. As often as not, the daydreams lead to reality. Whether or not I make the journey has everything to do with finding the time to make it happen and study as much as I can about what is needed to ascend. My consultations range from printed books and old maps, to the internet and word of mouth. After my research, I always formulate a plan of action. I do the things that are deemed necessary by those who have gone before me.

In all my years, I have never met a person who summited a mountain by mistake. In Dallas Willard's analysis, it takes vision, intention, and means.[5] After all, "it is not the mountain we conquer, but ourselves."[6] During this process of exploration, that conquering of self has proved to be an indispensable part of reaching a new peak. In a dynamic that I call "climber's curiosity," you reach a peak that you think is the last one of your journey, only to find that just beyond it is yet another peak a little higher and usually more technical. You are faced with the prospect of deciding whether or not to settle on the lower peak, analyzing whether or not the cost will outweigh the payoff.

Most climbers understand this curiosity will never allow us to settle on anything but the top. We must see what we are missing and so we press on. We are motivated to know every possible detail that is found on that further peak. And so it goes, peak after peak, in an endless cycle of constant

---

[5] Dallas Willard, *Renovation of the Heart*, (USA, NavPress, 2002).

[6] Edmund Hillary, quote from interview with Pittsburgh Post-Gazette, (1998).

striving, always pressing on to the next summit. This curiosity is best summed up in the words of the great mountaineer George Mallory who, when asked why he attempted multiple times to summit Mount Everest, responded simply, "Because it was there."[7]

I have found I am more than an explorer merely in a physical sense, but spiritually as well. Naturalist John Muir wrote in a letter to his sister in 1873, "The mountains are calling and I must go and I will work on while I can, studying incessantly."[8] In this statement, he captured the essence of my spiritual journey. Beyond this famous quote's tenure as a bumper sticker or a pithy T-shirt design, it serves as the basis of my commitment to live for Christ in the fullest manner possible. I want to go all-in on my spiritual journey while I can.

Even if, like Mallory, I never reach the highest peak, I am devoted to studying, digging deeper, and never settling for a lower spiritual peak. I will pursue it doggedly for the simple reason that it is there. For some explorers, it is about conquering and proving their physical prowess, but for me the prize is discovery. It is about acquiring knowledge that I did not have previously and would have never found had I not chosen to explore. This opportunity to explore, and as a result discover, warms my heart and sends my mind racing with possibilities.

---

[7] George Mallory, *The New Times*, (May 19, 1997), Section A, 14.

[8] John Muir, *Letter from John Muir to Sarah Muir Galloway*, (1873).

Explorers must explore

EVEN IF MY JOURNEY is a vicarious one, I celebrate this spirit of exploration and curiosity in others. I have long channeled the feeling through films and books. I never pass on the opportunity to watch an *Indiana Jones* flick. Sheepishly, I admit to being caught up in the spirit of adventure again recently while listening to an audiobook on a long trip. I hung on each paragraph of Douglas Preston's bestseller *The Lost City of the Monkey God.* His historical accounts of a rumored "Ciudad Blanca" or "White City" located in the deep and impenetrable jungles of the Central American nation of Honduras were riveting. The stories of what were and what could be enthralled me for each of the 10 or more hours of the book's run time. I felt it, too, while reading *The Lost City of Z* by David Grann, detailing Percy Fawcett's exploration of South America and the depths of the Amazon. Even classical literature that plunges me to the depths of J.R.R. Tolkien's Mordor or C.S. Lewis's Narnia has always piqued the desire to step through the cave or wardrobe and see what is on the other side; to see what is "further up and further in."

With so much to explore, it amazes me that there is a large swath of humans who find such opportunities uninviting, simply because of the risk involved. This group is content to sit on the ledge and look up and imagine what it is like on the summit. Yet because of their apprehension, they will never take steps to actually see the beauty or feel the fresh cold wind on their cheeks. Sadly, this will not only keep you off the summit of a mountain, but it can also lead you to a life of spiritual lethargy that looks nothing like what Jesus promised when he said, "I have come that you might have life, and have it to the full." [9]

This ho-hum existence is the root cause of despondency in our current Christian society. Explorer and priest Charles de Fouauld recognized this while living in the Algerian desert, concluding that "the absence of risk is a sure sign of mediocrity."[10] We congratulate ourselves on an "above average" lifestyle, failing to recognize that the designation only places us one small tick above mediocrity. And as a result, we are drowning in a pool of shallow and tepid water.

One can witness a similar attitude of comfortable contentment bordering on complete apathy on full display in the desert, in the Israelites' response to the report of Moses' Promised Land spies. The majority saw the risk as being too high. Only two found the possibilities endless and well worth the effort. The other 10 chose to live without risk and embraced the mediocrity that God had never intended for them. When we review the names found on the list in Numbers 13, we see Shammua, Shaphat, Igal, Palti,

---

[9] John 10:10, *Zondervan NIV Study Bible,* K. L. Barker, Ed.; Full rev. ed. (Zondervan, 2002).

[10] V.T. George, *His Silent Steps,* (St. Paul's, 2007), 148.

Gaddiel, Gaddi, Ammiel, Sethur, Nahbi, and Geuel, none of whom are ever mentioned again. Nor do they conjure up thoughts of an old Sunday School lesson. You likely never heard their names in a sermon. But, if I mention those who held out against the status quo, the narrative changes.

When we hear the names Caleb and Joshua most Christians have images of greatness, courage, and fulfillment, because these men were willing to explore, discover, and climb to the highest peak possible. Many parents go so far as to name their children after these men in hopes that they will embody the same spirit. One group stayed comfortable and the other pair pressed on. The former is forgotten and the latter is celebrated. It is safe to say that no one cares to remember mediocrity. In fact, we generally tend to flee from it as quickly as possible.

Pale by comparison

WHEN WE VIEW Jesus' aforementioned words in John 10:10 in a few modern versions of the Bible, we see that our understanding of the "full life" or "abundant life" is greatly hindered by our English language's limited ability to bring color to the text. In *The Message* translation of the Bible we see the way pastor/poet Eugene Peterson illuminates the passage when he translates it: "I came so they can have real and eternal life, more and better life than they ever dreamed of."[11] And then the technicolor Amplified Version states, "I came that they may have and enjoy life, and have it in abundance [to the full, till it overflows.]"[12] This is the life we were actually created to live. It is a life of risk but with even greater rewards, a life of being fully alive, and fully human. It is life as we were engineered to experience it when God first proclaimed, "Let Us make man in Our image."[13]

This promise of an overflowing and abundant life is demonstrated powerfully in the Parable of the Sower found in the Bible's synoptic Gospels: Matthew, Mark, and Luke. Jesus explained that the seed of the Word of God was sown in all four soils in a like manner, but with varying outcomes. The first seed sown along the path was immediately taken away by the enemy because of its hardness and inability to allow the seed to take root. Next, it was sown on rocky ground where it was received with joy. But problems — maybe Jesus was asking them for a little too much to become a true disciple — caused the rootless plant to die. Thirdly, it was sown among the thorns and basically "life happened." Business and success, cars and amenities — you name it — choked it out. Then the seeds finally fell on good soil.

---

[11] John 10:10, MSG
[12] John 10:10, AMP
[13] Genesis 1:26

Jesus taught his disciples that the good soil was an analogy for those who hear and understand the Word. This type of person hears and accepts that there is indeed more to life than what they were striving for or how they are currently living. This desire to explore the possibilities with God opened them up to a life that was 30, 60, and even 100 times greater than the way they lived. It refers to a life that is above and beyond the sum total of our talents, our senses, and our abilities. It is a full, abundant, real, and better life. Ultimately, it is a life that is ever-expanding and ever-growing. It is an exponential life.

During his life on earth, this agrarian metaphor would have been so readily understood simply because everyone was a farmer or had a farm that provided their food. Today these words can be lost on us if we do not take a moment to step back into a time before fossil- fuel tractors, steel plows, synthetic fertilizers, and overfilled produce sections in a local grocery store. It was a time when everything was organic; an age when the carbon footprint of a farmer solely depended on the size of the animal's hoof they were plowing with, and their work was done out of necessity rather than hobby.

Many will relegate this amazing text to nothing more than a cliché or a cross stitch that is framed and crammed into a dark corner of their house. It is worthwhile to at least attempt to grasp it on the level recognized by those who heard it 2,000 years ago. At the time of its telling, the meaning was so self-evident that, unlike the Parable of the Sower, it required no private explanation for the disciples. For us to fully understand what Jesus is hoping to communicate here, it is best to break down what he was saying. Anyone who reads this can clearly see that he makes three simple invitations to his disciples. He invites them to come, take, and learn.

Regrettably, for most of us the exponential life promised by Jesus is a rare occurrence. But just because it is a scarcity in our modern churches does not mean it does not exist or it isn't attainable. Consider the narwhal. Who would have thought that a whale with a unicorn tusk protruding from its head could be anything but another branch on the fairy tale tree alongside mermaids, leprechauns, and Bigfoot? Although rare and bordering on extinction, narwhals do indeed exist. So it is with followers of Christ who take him at his word and determine to enter into his promised, exponential life.

Amid the outpouring of parables in Matthew 13, Jesus offers more insight into this full life he promised. Immediately following the Parable of the Sower, we find in short order a handful of teachings that use seeds, yeast, treasure, and pearls to illustrate the Kingdom's effect on us when we fully take hold of it. From these parables, I have taken four simple questions that shed light on our souls and allow us to see what's really going on in our unexplored depths.

First, consider the mustard seed (vv. 31-32). Are you growing? Exponential life grows eternally. It never arrives and it never tops out. It is not a destination, but an organic journey. Second, Jesus conjures the image of yeast (v. 33). Ask yourself, is your life being permeated by your relationship with Jesus? Yeast overtakes and reaches into every corner of the dough it touches, and so should Jesus' words into your life. Once it becomes active, permeation is inevitable. Third, the promised Kingdom is like a treasure (v. 44). Are you seeking his Kingdom with the same fervor that you would seek out a buried treasure, knowing full well it is of much more value eternally? Finally, Jesus uses a "pearl of great price" (vv. 45-46). The pearl is of immense value to the one who found it, so much so that he was willing to sacrifice everything to acquire it. What are you sacrificing for your pearl of great price?

Now ask yourself if your current spiritual state reflects the exponential promise that Jesus made to those who would be his disciples. Does it have the characteristics mentioned above? Is it growing? Is it permeating every corner of your life? Are you seeking it as a treasure? Are you willing to sacrifice everything to acquire it? Or is it more of a shallow, empty, lacking, get-by, make-do, hold-on-'til-payday existence that is wrapped around merely getting what you think you want? A *Washington Times* article gives an answer for most American Christians with a recent headline. It reads: "America's New Religion: Fake Christianity."[14]

The article makes a distinction between a true, biblical, and vibrant Christianity and a recent Christian mutation called Moralistic Therapeutic Deism (MTD). Researcher George Barna defined MTD like this:

> The moralistic perspective is we're here to be good people and to try to do good. The therapeutic aspect is everything is supposed to be geared to making me feel good about myself, ultimately to make me happy. Deism is the idea that God created the world but has no direct involvement in it. Basically, according to MTD, there is a distant God who just wants everyone to be nice, and the purpose of life is to be happy. American 'Christians' who have adopted this philosophy have elevated[d] personal definitions of right and wrong above any objective standard of Truth — like the Bible.[15]

There are an inordinate number of people in our society and in our churches who believe Jesus came to make them comfortable and happy. This mentality persists in spite of an inability to point to these ideas anywhere in his preaching. Regardless, they have become the bedrock of our mod-

[14] Piper, E. *America's New Religion: Fake Christianity*. The Washington Times. (2021, July 25)

[15] Ibid.

ern message and it is leading us to an ever deeper pit of mediocre despair.

When I compare Jesus' promise of an exponential life with our current reality — which seems to be increasingly risk-averse in the church — I find that the latter pales in comparison to the former. Remember, first and foremost, Jesus proclaimed that he had come to give life. We see this life throughout the Church's history from generation to generation, at times burning with the flames of revival and at other times flickering in the desert or in caves. Usually, as with the modern church, the greatest enemy standing between us and an exponential life is our desire for comfort and happiness.

Remember, the quality of the seed is of no use if we (the soil receiving the seed) refuse to let go of the idol of personal gratification. Our obsession with this pursuit has neutered the gospel and made it something it was never intended to be. This has historically been the case. Many are now content to coexist with a religion the apostle Paul warned Timothy to avoid (2 Tim. 3:5). It's the sort of religion that while "having a form of godliness" (all the right words spoken at the right time), nevertheless denies its power. Or as John the Beloved saw in the church of Laodicea, a church that God rebuked because it was "neither hot nor cold, but lukewarm."[16] This is a description of a church and a religion

[16] Revelation 3:15

where nothing is exponential. There exists an incapability of changing the world and even a hopelessness to transform a single life.

Road map

AT THIS JUNCTURE, you may find yourself in one of the three positions common to those who hear stories about the exponential life. If you are more worried about the possibility of losing the known but temporary comfort of your day-to-day existence in favor of the exponential life, you hold this fear to your own detriment. This posture is dangerous as Augustine of Hippo explained more than 16 centuries ago:

> The strength of self-deceivers is not that strength that well people enjoy, but like those in delirium. They are like those out of their minds, who imagine themselves in such good health that they do not consult a physician, and even fall upon him with blows as if he were an intruder! In the same way, these delirious people, with their mad pride, fall upon Christ with blows, so to speak, because they have felt no need of his kindly help to those who seek to be just according to the prescriptions of the law. Let them, then, put away this madness. Let them understand, as far as they are able, that they have free

> will, and that they are called not to despise the Lord's help with a proud heart, but to call upon him with a contrite heart. The free will then will be free in proportion as it is sound, and sound in proportion as it is submissive to divine mercy and grace.[17]

In all your cringing and hesitating, you cannot see or imagine the untold spiritual riches you will find as a result. Your fear and apprehension will freeze your efforts and leave you admitting that the cost is simply too high.

Others of you are like me, explorers by nature. You are among those who have never refrained from jeopardizing your own personal wishes and wants. You have learned to look suspiciously at the idols of individual comfort and happiness, knowing from the bottom of your heart they are not protecting us, but keeping us from a full life. You know that in some way, shape, or form that when God came in the flesh through Jesus in the Incarnation — when he walked a mile in humanity's shoes — he may have left us more insight into this thing we call life than we currently possess. This group is motivated by the climber's curiosity that always wants to know what lies further up and further in and a desire to catch the view from the highest peak you can find, whatever the price.

---

[17] Oden, Thomas, *Ancient Christian Commentary on Scripture, New Testament II, Mark,* (InterVarsity Press, 2014), 30.

Here we have two completely opposite, but realistic, views of the same opportunity: those who shudder at Jesus' invitation to "give up their life, so that they might find it"[18] and those who paw the ground in anticipation of what awaits. U.S. President Abraham Lincoln offered us a timeless perspective when he noted, "We can complain because rose bushes have thorns, or rejoice because thorn bushes have roses."[19] If we are to pursue the exponential life we must put our fear of the thorns aside and celebrate the beauty of the multitude of roses that miraculously grow among the thorns of life.

The third group may well be the largest. These are the ones who find themselves in neither camp, but instead feel stuck in their journey toward Jesus' promise of an overflowing life. As a result, they find themselves doing nothing wrong, but also doing nothing right. Their situation has caused them to simply stop making an effort. They neither ascend nor descend what is before them. Their home is in the slough of confusion where frustration abounds. Internally, they may hear a voice that whispers *you are actually better off settling*. I have to admit I have found myself in this place in the past. I didn't know what to do and found it safer to sit still rather than risk worsening the situation. I soon

---

[18] Matthew 16:25

[19] *Wilderness Wisdom: Quotes for Inspirational Exploration*, (NOLS: National Outdoor Leadership School), Edited by John Gookin, (Stackpole Books, 2003), 79.

found that this response to the opportunity only leads to the mediocrity and lukewarmness that Jesus so adamantly warns us about.

The etymology of the word *mediocrity* tells the story. It is formed from the Latin words for "middle" and "rugged mountain." It connotes stopping when the going gets too tough. In those times I have found that one way forward is to seek out someone who is ahead of me in their journey and humbly ask for input to continue moving forward. It is almost always slow and tedious. I needed to crawl before I could walk. Sometimes, we suffer indignities for the sake of continuing the climb. Explorers come in all shapes and sizes, but I have yet to meet one who would not stop for a moment to lend some advice to others, even when it meant a minor delay in their own plans.

If you have never truly lived, the fear of death can be an almost insurmountable obstacle. This is a travesty because he is calling every one of his followers, including you, to summit the peaks of this promised exponential life. But you must choose to do it. It is something more than wishing, hoping, or imagining. It is consciously determining to prepare your pack. It means studying the course and the lives of others who have taken on this same promise, and training yourself through consistent and intense self-discipline. I invite you to come explore with me, not because I have achieved the highest peaks, but because I have the same desire. Maybe all you can do right now is crawl. Just make the same choice the great missionary and explorer David Livingstone did when he proclaimed, "I'll go anywhere provided that it be forward."[20]

To those who are pawing the ground and to those who are stuck, the following chapters are for you. The principles ahead are not infallible, but they are substantiated by a "great crowd of witnesses" that has gone before us. They do not live and breathe, but can guide and direct. They can open the door to unknown possibilities and breakthroughs. They will lead you to vistas and views and to discoveries and explorations that will allow you to wade ever deeper into the full exponential of the life Jesus promised you. To those who roll their eyes at the notion of pursuing the full possibilities of what God has promised when he announced that he had fulfilled the words of the prophet Isaiah in Luke 4 and to spiritual skeptics: I ask that each of you consider the Chinese proverb as you fall in with whichever approach you so choose in this life: "The person who says it cannot be done should not interrupt the person who is doing it."[21]

---

[20] *David Livingstone: Pathfinder,* The Outlook Volume 103, (Princeton University, 1913), 585.

[21] James Egan, *1000 Inspiring Quotes*, (Lulu, 2015), 109.

Make it personal

1. As a Christian, can I identify differences in my life from those of my non-Christian neighbors?

2. What comforts am I afraid to lose in pursuit of the exponential life?

3. In the past year, what significant changes can I point to in my life to suggest progress in spiritual growth?

2. The Exponential Life

IN AN AGE of mass-produced media that generally lack anything remotely resembling personal or heartfelt sentiment, a handwritten letter or postcard speaks volumes. It grabs your attention and makes you lay aside the rest of the printed rabble that fills your postbox each day. You take a few moments to intimately engage with the one who personally thought of you. Perhaps the only correspondence that can trump the beauty of a letter is a personal invitation from a close friend.

Such an invitation is categorically different from the majority of our recycled print or those awkward moments of social obligation wherein an impending gathering for which you've not made the guest list is brought to your attention and, as a result, the host feels compelled to tell you to come along assuring you that there will be enough room. Far from it, the invitation I am referring to happens when a close friend calls you to make sure you're at home and then swings by to specifically invite you to be a part of something special. Such opportunities are not generally declined.

We find one of these life-changing invitations in Matthew 11. Jesus beautifully extends an opportunity to his disciples as well as to us. He proclaims:

> Come unto me, all ye that labor and are heavy laden, and I will give you rest. Take my yoke upon you, and learn of me; for I am meek and lowly in heart: and ye shall find rest unto your souls. For my yoke is easy, and my burden is light.[22]

This is an invitation to enter into and to live every day in his Kingdom. It is one that leads us to the overflowing and exponential life referred to in John 10:10.

Come unto me

JESUS OPENELY INVITES US by proclaiming, "Come unto me, all ye that labor and are heavy laden, and I will give you rest." It starts with our movement toward Jesus and our response to the realization that "the Word was made flesh, and dwelt among us."[23] It is our affirmative reply to the Incarnation's knocking on the door of our life. Revelation 3:20 demonstrates that this knocking is actively taking place, even now as you are reading. Jesus proclaimed, "Behold, I stand at the door, and knock: if any man hears my voice, and opens the door I will come in to him, and will sup with him, and he with me." It is the

[22] Matthew 11:28-30, KJV
[23] John 1:14

groundbreaking acknowledgment that comes when we finally understand more clearly what it means that our Creator is everywhere and present rather than a God who is distant and removed. Most of us who have struggled with the notion of a God who feels far away do so subconsciously without admitting it to themselves. To acknowledge the feeling makes way for the fear of being put out of our fellowships or churches. But our actions in life and maybe even more so our interactions with God reveal our true beliefs more than our stale creedal proclamations.

He is knocking. The maker of all time and matter is closer than the breath in your lungs and he is inviting you to open the doors of your life so that you may know him even more. This invitation to come is not extended to every Tom, Dick, and Harry, but only to those who labor and feel a heavy burden. "In any moment of decision, the best thing you can do is the right thing, the next best thing is the wrong thing, and the worst thing you can do is nothing."[24] The invitation is for those who are trying to do it right, even as they are doing it wrong. Although Jesus compassionately cried out to those who are struggling, he never attempted to lull us into a false sense of security that somehow he invited us to a life of leisure and ease. It is an invitation to those who are making attempts at doing the right thing, even when they may be off track in their attempts.

---

[24] Quote commonly attributed to Theodore Roosevelt.

I love to hear someone start a conversation that concerns spiritual matters with the phrase, "I'm struggling to do X" or "I am having a hard time with Y." Your admission of struggle indicates that you are living and trying, and not yet dead. You could read this first invitation of Jesus this way: "Come to me all you strugglers." Are you struggling? Hear your Savior's persistent knocking on the door of your life, open the door, and let him inside. It is a step of giving him full access, because your plans are not working out the way you intended and you need direction. We must be willing to allow him in, even when we are unsure of what exactly he is up to.

This opening of the door is the ultimate understanding of repentance. It's the humble recognition that there is a better way of doing something and deciding to change your method as a result. This invitation is to the explorers who realize they are climbing the wrong path or maybe even the wrong mountain and it is time to correct their trajectory.

For me it took place in 2008 when I realized that I was living and striving toward my own metrics of success. My goals were such that they could only be achieved by giving up my peace and working at a rapid pace to make sure all the boxes were constantly checked. My marriage suffered, my family suffered, I suffered and ultimately my relationship with God suffered. I realized the grief I was causing my Heavenly Father when I finally grasped that God had called me to be fruitful, not successful. It was only when I had achieved a certain level of this success in the eyes of the world that I understood my mistake.

This included things I thought would make everything better: the recognition of my name and accomplishments in print and film; the overwhelming number of invitations extended to speak at numerous churches and events; the overfilled venues I addressed each week; the dozens of buildings constructed; the money raised. It all became instantly hollow. When I realized that God had never called me to be what I had determined to be classified as successful, my human accomplishments seemed every bit the "filthy rags," the prophet Isaiah assessed as his so-called righteous acts. I was, as C. S. Lewis put it, aiming for earth instead of heaven and in the process getting neither.[25]

I found myself on the summit of a fictitious spiritual mountain where the peaks were numerical church growth, perfection in weekly presentations, and performance for the consumers who attended. From the beginning, when I started to climb, it sure looked like the truth to me. When I reached the top of the summit, I found out that not only was it not what I thought it would be, I had the painful realization that I wasn't even on the right mountain!

In a moment of extreme clarity, I recognized that Jesus had told me what would honor the Father and it wasn't

---

[25] Original quote, "Aim at Heaven and you will get earth "thrown in," aim at earth and you will get neither." C. S. Lewis, *Mere Christianity*, (Harper Collins, 2001), 134.

success as I measured it. Instead, it was becoming fruitful in the things that mattered to him. The Amplified Bible presents the words of Jesus like this: "My Father is glorified and honored by this, when you bear much fruit, and prove yourselves to be My [true] disciples."[26] Theologian Henri Nouwen understood this when he wrote, "We are called to be fruitful — not successful, not productive, not accomplished. Success comes from strength, stress, and human effort. Fruitfulness comes from vulnerability and the admission of our own weakness."[27]

I arrived at the crossroads common to those who realize such an error and with my arrival came a question: Would I continue in the same direction I had always gone and hope for a different outcome, or would I repent and change course? It wasn't an easy choice, because no one likes to admit he is wrong even when no one else is around. This is especially hard for leaders with hundreds of followers.

It is a humbling gesture to truly repent, to tear down the very wall you have worked to build. I knew that my ego would take a hit when I announced that we had been on the wrong course. I would once again prove to everyone that I was not infallible and inevitably — when left to my own devices — I could and would make mistakes. It would require a period of disassembly, of rebuilding and a lot of

---

[26] John 15:8

[27] Paul Hargreaves, *The Fourth Bottom Line: Flourishing in a New Age of Compassionate Leadership,* (SRA Books, 2021), quote from Day 18.

slow, methodical shifts to change the direction of my life. It was during this time that I recognized a rather difficult truth. When you begin the process of repentance, the level of your pain is usually determined by the height of the platform you have built for yourself.

This process is so painful that it can only be overcome by humility, which is the key to unlocking the grace you need to make it through. As both the epistles of Peter and James remind us, "God resists the proud, but gives grace to the humble."[28] When humility is embraced it will only multiply God's grace in our lives. Humility has always been the required characteristic needed to start the process of realizing you were wrong and rectifying the error.

By the grace of God, I chose the path of repentance, not because I had sinned, but because there was a better way. I threw open the doors and windows of my life. I gave access to the depths of my being to the God I had invited into my life almost 20 years before. In the process, I learned of the importance of the unseen life and digging deeper before moving forward. In the words of Augustine, I found solace in realizing that in the basement of my being I was doing the greatest work of my life:

> If you wish to reach high, then begin at the lowest level. If you are trying to construct some mighty edifice in

---

[28] James 4:6-7, 1 Peter 5:5-6

> height, you will begin with the lowest foundation. This is humility. However great the mass of the building you may wish to design or erect, the taller the building is to be, the deeper you will dig the foundation.[29]

The repentance, the tearing down what is out of place and learning to live life at a different rhythm, proved to be a tedious process. At times, I did nothing more than crawl, but I have learned when I can do nothing else, crawling is enough as long as my journey is upward. The older I become, the more I have learned to live with the reminder, "it is never too late to be what you might have been."[30]

Take my yoke

IT IS IMPORTANT to see the context of Jesus' invitation. It is not open-ended or sappy. It is extended to those who are willing to climb in pursuit of him. This beautiful reality is seen in Eugene Peterson's description of what preceded the Sermon on the Mount. "When Jesus saw his ministry drawing huge crowds, he climbed a hillside. Those who were apprenticed to him, the committed, climbed with him. Arriving at a quiet place, he sat down and taught his

---

[29] Manlio Simonetti, *Ancient Christian Commentary on Scripture: Matthew 1-13*, (InterVarsity Press, 2014), Matthew 11:28-29.
[30] Quote commonly attributed to George Eliot.

climbing companions."[31] This should never be viewed as ambiguous. As you take time to listen to his words, it becomes apparent they are very specific.

Again, this invitation is not to a cake walk nor to a place on easy street. An invitation to take on his yoke is a call to work with him, not to sit back and enjoy the ride. Jesus never promised that the exponential life would be without difficulty, but rather the contrary. In Luke 13:24, his disciples asked him a question about the possibility of salvation and Jesus told them to "strive to enter in at the narrow gate." Even so, he doesn't expect us to do it alone. He invites us to connect ourselves to his unlimited grace and power through his yoke. The exponential life comes as a result of making the decision to work *with* God, instead of against him.

His listeners would have known the function and use of a yoke. It was as common as a car today. Every farmer and farm had at least one. It was used to increase productivity. Most of the time two animals would work side by side in order to carry a load that one could not do alone. Typically a young, untrained ox or horse would be yoked with an older, trained animal. The younger is intended to learn from its proximity to the older.

Statistically, a trained draft horse can pull 8,000 pounds and an untrained draft horse can pull 4,000 pounds. Logic

[31] Matthew 5:1-2, MSG

tells me, then, that together they can pull 12,000 pounds. Yet over time, the untrained draft horse becomes trained and the two begin to walk in-step with each other. Eventually in an ideal in-step scenario they can each pull 8,000 pounds respectively. Yet if I ask you the sum total of their collective abilities, general math would tell you that amount would be 16,000 pounds. Surprisingly, that is not the case. Exponentially those two horses can pull 24,000 pounds.[32] I believe that Jesus knew this far before agricultural science confirmed it. This is a window into what it truly means to live an exponential life. As a work animal learns to pull and increases its ability, eventually it reaches a point where the production of the two animals is greater than the sum of its total. Each animal added to the yoke would thereby increase its power even more.

It is basically growth that is duplicated and that speeds up over time. Look what happens when you take 10 to the fourth power.

10x10=100
100x10=1000
1000x10=10,000
10,000x10=100,000

---

[32] Stovall, J. (2012, January 16). *Horse Sense.* Tim Maurer. Retrieved from https://timmaurer.com/2012/01/16/horse-sense/.

The total would continue to increase as long as the equation was kept alive. It increases *exponentially*. In the same way, our yoking to Jesus brings with it a promise of ever expanding capacity to truly live life as it was intended to be lived. It is there, beside him, that we learn how to live our lives as image bearers, the life for which we were created. Over time, we will catch his rhythm that permits us to live in step with the Trinity and as a result, our growth curve angles up and up so that it produces what can only be classified as the exponential life.

Jesus' invitation to join his master class of true living is to all the strugglers who will take on his yoke. I have made much of the fact that this summons will not result in a painless life, to which you might well reply, "But when Jesus presents his yoke, it's as one that is both 'easy' and 'light.'" It is a common error for our 21st-century minds to be led astray by these descriptors. We read this as if somehow we are being invited to enjoy some type of spiritual lazy river where you simply "let go and let God."

"The spiritual life is a gift. It is a gift of the Holy Spirit, who lifts us up into the kingdom of God's love. But to say that being lifted up into the kingdom of love is a divine gift does not mean that we wait passively until the gift is offered to us."[33]

---

[33] Henry Nouwen, *Making All Things New*, (Harper Collins, 2009), 65-68.

Jesus' use of this word *easy* has nothing to do with our attempt, as if he were calling us to a life of apathetic existence. It is easy in the sense that it fits us perfectly. It was made for us because we are created in His image. And when we see the word *light* it should be understood to mean that this yoke is highly effective. It does not remove the burden nor does it eliminate the weight of our lives, but rather makes it feel much lighter when it is well-placed on our shoulders.

Yoking ourselves with Christ is a commitment to yield our lives to his way of life. We are like cars with a warped frame, constantly pulling in the wrong direction and in need of correcting. His yoke is there to keep us on the right path. If we yield ourselves to our sinful and carnal nature, we cannot help but to run a warped path. If left unattended, this drift will leave us on a perpendicular path to his truth. Have you ever wondered how a man or woman of God could wander so far from the grace that God had bestowed upon him or her? It usually starts with the decision to walk away from Jesus' yoke after somehow being convinced to do it their own way. Thus they exchange the easy yoke that makes their burdens lighter — the one for which they were created — and in its place take on another malformed yoke, one that is difficult and makes their lives heavier than they were designed to be.

Did I miss something?

IT IS IMPORTANT to note here that Jesus is not talking about earning salvation through works. We can hear echoes of this invitation in the Sermon on the Mount:

> Enter by the narrow gate; for wide is the gate and broad is the way that leads to destruction, and there are many who go in by it. Because narrow is the gate and difficult is the way which leads to life, and there are few who find it.[34]

Augustine commented on this text in the fifth century:

> He says this not because the Lord's yoke is rough or his burden heavy, but because there are a few who wish their labors to end. They do not put their full trust in the Lord when he cries, "Come to me, all you who labor, and I will give you rest. Take my yoke upon you, and learn from me, for I am meek and humble of heart. For my yoke is easy, and my burden is light."[35]

The gate is narrow because it requires you trusting Jesus and his understanding of life. It is hard because it asks you

---

[34] Matthew 7:12-14

[35] Augustine, *Commentary on the Lord's Sermon on the Mount with Seventeen Related Sermons*, (CUA, 2010), 188.

to give up control and to follow him. If salvation could somehow be earned, it would mean that his death on the cross would have been a wasted gesture. Every person who has truly heard the good news knows unequivocally that salvation comes only due to the grace that God extends to all sinners. We recognize and receive that grace through faith.

Too many misunderstand the grace we are afforded. This in turn leads to mediocrity, lethargy, and the belief there is nothing to do but to hang on until heaven. As Dallas Willard explained, "Grace is not opposed to effort, it is opposed to earning."[36] The idea that spiritual depth could come through osmosis or as the result of a solitary act is nothing more than a fallacy on par with a retirement plan based on the leprechaun's gold found at the end of the rainbow. It will only become reality through protracted effort that includes a perpetual commitment to personal correction. It is following in the steps of those who have gone before us. This sentiment is highlighted in Hebrews 6:12,[37] "that you do not become [lazy] sluggish, but imitate those who through faith and patience inherit the promises." It will require both faith and its twin brother patience.

We do well to follow the example of the apostle Paul in his letter to the Philippian church: "Not that I have already

---

[36] Dallas Willard, *The Great Omission: Reclaiming Jesus's Teaching on Discipleship*, (Harper Collins, 2006), 34.

[37] KJV

attained, or am already perfected; but I press on, that I may lay hold of that for which Christ Jesus has also laid hold of me."[38] It is taking Jesus at his word that his kingdom is truly at hand and dwells within each of us. The image we were created in — the image of our Creator — may be like a speck of leaven, unnoticeable to the observing eye. It may lie in wait like a treasure that is buried under years of sin, selfishness, resentments, rebellions, unforgiveness, wishes, and wants. Although it is hidden and tarnished, it is still there and worth more than any jewel ever found. We are not striving to get into the kingdom of God, but to nurture what God is doing in our lives, to allow it to overtake every corner of our being, to make sure that it is transforming our being and, in the process, making it real in our families, communities, and in the lives of others.

Early Church father John Chrysostom reminds us that the effort becomes delightful when we take time to see what it is leading us toward. He wrote:

> It is not only on the way that the things of excellence become easy. In the end they become even more agreeable. For it is not just the passing away of toil and sweating, but also the anticipated arrival at a pleasant destina-

[38] Philippians 3:12-14

> tion that is sufficient to encourage the traveler. For this road ends in life! [39]

When we keep the promise in plain view, the blood, sweat, and tears that will be part of our endeavor to live it out will appear as nothing more than temporal inconveniences on the road to the life God created us to live: the exponential life.

When we accept Jesus' invitation to come, it leads us to the headwaters of the exponential life. The apostle Paul lived this life. He had taken on the yoke, and as a result he inspired others to take on the climb in Ephesians 3:19-20.[40] He encouraged them to, "know the love of Christ, which passeth knowledge, that ye might be filled with all the fullness of God. Now unto him that is able to do exceeding abundantly above all that we ask or think, according to the power that worketh in us." This exceeding abundance was nothing less than Paul's way of saying *exponential.*

Learn from me

THIS INVITATION to allow God access into your life should not be seen as an offer for a type of celestial house-

---

[39] Manlio Simonetti, *Ancient Christian Commentary on Scripture: Matthew 1-13*, (InterVarsity Press, 2014), Matthew 7:13-14.

[40] KJV

keeping service that will come in and clean up all little messes that have been caused by the wrong things you have been attempting to do. We take on the yoke as opposed to "kicking against the goads," as Paul confessed to doing in Acts 26:14[41] prior to his conversion on the road to Damascus. Many learn the hard way that they cannot out-run their problems, mainly because the greatest instigator in our lives is the person that looks back at us when we stare into a mirror. If we cannot run from our problems, what can we do? We can run toward the answer.

This exponential life comes as a result of making the decision to work with God, instead of against him. Our surrender is more akin to a supernatural extreme makeover that breaks down the wrong and fixes it by replacing it with the right things; the things you were created to do.

> Imagine yourself as a living house. God comes in to rebuild that house. At first, perhaps, you can understand what He is doing. He is getting the drains right and stopping the leaks in the roof and so on; you knew that those jobs needed doing and so you are not surprised. But presently He starts knocking the house about in a way that hurts abominably and does not seem to make any sense. What on earth is He up to? The explanation is that He is building quite a different house from the

---

[41] KJV

> one you thought of — throwing out a new wing here, putting on an extra floor there, running up towers, making courtyards. You thought you were being made into a decent little cottage: but He is building a palace. He intends to come and live in it Himself. [42]

This can be daunting when the walls are being ripped out, but as C. S. Lewis found out, it is a matter of faith, which is nothing more than simple trust. We must believe that God has better plans for us than we have for ourselves.

Jesus' yoke is not a pain-free existence, but it is straightforward and simple. Committing to walk the path of our Lord toward an exponential life doesn't in any way serve as a get-out-of-jail-free card which renders us impervious to the unavoidable storms of life. It promises only the stability to weather the storms as they come. Jesus assured us of this reality in Matthew 7:24-25:

> Therefore whoever hears these sayings of Mine, and does them, I will liken him to a wise man who built his house on the rock: and the rain descended, the floods came, and the winds blew and beat on that house; and it did not fall, for it was founded on the rock.

[42] CS Lewis, *Mere Christianity*, (HarperCollins, 1952), 175-176.

We are attempting to embody our belief in order to become men and women who are fully alive.

In the second century, Irenaeus compared it to listening to the advice of your doctor whom you trust to cure what ails you.

> What competent doctor, when asked to cure a sick person, would simply follow the desires of the patient, and not act in accordance with the requirements of good medicine? The Lord himself testified that he came as the physician of the sick, saying, "Those who are well have no need of a physician, but those who are sick; I came not to call the righteous, but sinners." How, then, are the sick to be made strong? How are sinners to repent? Is it by merely holding fast to what they are presently doing? Or, on the contrary, by undergoing a great change and reversal of their previous behavior, by which they had brought upon themselves serious illness and many sins? Ignorance, the mother of intractability, is driven out by knowing the truth. Therefore the Lord imparted knowledge of the truth to his disciples, by which he cured those who were suffering, and restrained sinners from sin. So he did not speak to them in accordance with their previous assumptions, nor answer ac-

> cording to the presumptions of inquirers, but according to sound teaching, without any pretense or pandering. [43]

We must apply what we say we believe into our everyday lives or, like an unopened and unused bottle of medicine, it is of little benefit. These truths that Irenaeus referred to are not some hidden enigmas that must be ascertained in secret conversations in hushed halls, but they are in essence principles that must be recognized, discerned, and applied frequently if they are to be of any use.

The biblical texts we must use are not obscure, nor do they require an advanced degree in theology to embrace and apply. We are simply searching for the imperatives Jesus shared with his disciples by examining the gospel record. Rather than a plain reading, I encourage you to imagine that you are panning for gold, sifting and shifting, again and again, as you search the words and actions of our guide. Along the way, we must keep an eye out for those things he deemed vitally important, keeping in mind that not all commandments are created equal.

It will become clear that some are explicitly defined in plain language, while others are implicitly modeled through Jesus' habitual actions. These are the things he taught and modeled when he called fishermen, tax collectors, shepherds, prostitutes, divorcees, and farmers to follow him.

---

[43] Thomas C. Oden, Christopher A. Hall, *Ancient Christian Commentary on Scripture: Mark*, (InterVarsity Press, 2014), 29.

"But let us be assured that we are His brethren and His sisters, if we do the will of the Father; that we may be joint heirs with Him, for He discerns us not by sex [gender] but by our deeds."[44] It is intended for all of us as well, regardless of the label our life may have placed on us as a result of our perceived successes or our failures. As we commit to apply what we believe into our daily lives in our pursuit of truly living, let us rest assured that although the task is not free from effort, Jesus never intended for it to be complicated. Yet it is almost never instinctively easy.

Make it personal

1. How do you measure success? Does your metric seem in line or opposed to that which God would use?

2. Are there areas of your life in which you've abandoned effort or left unattended while asking God to do the work for you?

3. Are there good deeds or habits that you appeal to when you consider whether or not you are righteous in the eyes of God?

---

[44] Jerome, *Catena Aurea: St. Mark*, (John Henry Parker, 1842), 70.

3. On-Ramps to the Exponential Life

OVER THE COURSE of my personal pilgrimage, I realized that seeking answers to every question I had was not the best use of my time. I researched, studied, and learned only to remain frustrated, because the answer did not satisfy me. The issue wasn't in the truth of the answers, but in my own misguided questions. Several years ago, I made the decision to reprioritize my search, exchanging my effort for right answers with one for right questions. If you don't solve the problem of the question first, the hunt for answers will inevitably end in frustration, when you fail to find the magical pill or the silver bullet. The right questions have the power to take you places.

It's vital to pause and allow ourselves to sort through the questions that the first chapters present: Do you truly want this full, abundant, and exponential life that Jesus promised to his followers? Do you really want to know what it means to be an image bearer? Do you want everything Jesus offered when he proclaimed "the kingdom of heaven is at hand"?[45] Are you willing to fully embrace the journey that he offers, regardless of the destination? Do you really want

[45] Matthew 4:17

to be "made well"?[46] I pray that you are convinced that Jesus is indeed inviting you to live this life that he promised to his disciples. I hope that this conviction is leading you to accept that invitation, and once you do, that you would have the courage to repent, to surrender to his yoke that is easy and light, and ultimately to take your seat in his master class so that you can learn how to truly live as you were created to live.

If you accept his invitation to the exponential life, your first order of business is to lean heavily into the life and teachings of Jesus, his disciples, and the New Testament apostles. As we reflect on the imperatives, both explicit and implicit, we are taking on his yoke. Most have called these spiritual disciplines, and that is the form in which I initially encountered them.

As much as I respect the phrase and see its place in our need for formation, I found myself tripping over the terminology, as it reminded me of my childhood of being raised in a military family. The idiom conjured up thoughts of lock-stepped mindless tin soldiers marching to the beat of an unknown drummer. When taken at face value, it suggests eternal consequences for missing a roll call or veering off track with our spiritual calorie count. Without attempting to reinvent the wheel, I prefer to call these on-ramps like those found on an expressway or interstate.

[46] John 5:6

What is an on-ramp? Merriam-Webster defines it as "a ramp by which one enters a limited-access highway."[47] In the same way, these paradoxical imperatives allow us to enter into limited access or "straight and narrow" ways that lead to exponential life. These on-ramps allow us to merge from where we are to where we, as image bearers, were created to become.

I want to clarify what these on-ramps are and what they are not. An on-ramp by definition is never an end in itself; it should never be seen as an obligation, but an opportunity. On-ramps are always a means. In them, "we should not expect to find magical methods, systems which will make all the difficulties and obstacles dissolve into thin air."[48] It is simply a connector from where you are to where you want to go. You will find many highways that are memorialized and celebrated, but not on-ramps. You may hear of a vacation along Route 66, but you wouldn't think about a vacation on an on-ramp. I don't think I have ever heard of a book, song, or poem that attempted to memorialize exit 343 on Interstate Highway 65.

On-ramps are necessary and integral, but are not to be seen as destinations in and of themselves. You shouldn't let yourself get caught stopping on the on-ramp. Like grace,

---

[47] Merriam-Webster Online Dictionary, https://www.merriam-webster.com/dictionary/on-ramp

[48] Thomas Merton, *Contemplative Prayer*, (Image Books, 2014), 10.

on-ramps also offer an opportunity to correct your missed turns. They allow us the place and the space we need to turn around when we know we have veered off our desired course. Some achieve their function through being applied to just a short interval in our weekly lives and others may require quite a bit more time before the desired results are felt. Ultimately, on-ramps are there to get us pointed in the right direction, a destination that God has determined will lead us toward an exponential life.

As we journey, you will begin to realize that this yoke, like any yoke, requires tension to operate. It cannot function without it. As we walk ever deeper down this path we will feel the pull, first against our warped carnal nature. But we also will start to see that there is a positive type of tension that is being formed in our lives. It is the paradoxical nature of living in obedience to Jesus' imperatives. This paradox creates tension, and the tension in turn creates something powerful in our lives.

Our world is filled with paradoxes. A cursory look around will reveal a number of adages and principles which appear contradictory, yet — after a bit of analyzing — make all the sense in the world. We have all heard that we are to "save money, by spending it," "less is more," and "the only constant is change." There are no shortage of paradoxes in idioms.

When Jesus was asked to name the greatest commandment, he responded in Matthew 22:40, that it was loving

God and loving your neighbor as yourself. How can you do both and not sacrifice the other? Yet Jesus said these two paradoxical commandments to love would not cancel out each other, but generate enough strength and space on which we could confidently hang all of the "law and the prophets." As an ancient commentator noted, this paradox created a powerful tension: "Lest we fall into unholy doctrines, we must love God; so that we do not lead a corrupt life, we must love our neighbor. So by means of each other these two commandments are welded together and united, containing within themselves all the other commandments."[49]

Jesus described the gate to enter eternity as both narrow and at the same time large enough to accommodate whosoever would enter it. This tension is perhaps most clearly exhibited in the Trinity. How can God simultaneously be three persons and only one God? We see it again as the apostles Paul and James attempt to express the coexistence of faith and works in the Christian's life. We resolve this tension by replacing our either/or mentality and fully embracing a both/and approach. Most prefer to ignore or diminish views that don't fit their preset talking points in an attempt to eliminate the tension altogether, while God expects us to live somewhere in the middle of that tension.

[49] Theophylact of Ochrid, *The Explanation*, (Chrysostom Press, 1992), 193.

I realized that these on-ramps were leading me to very practical, concrete destinations in my spiritual life: destinations that would become just as real as the ground I stand on. These destinations seem to reflect the fruit of the Spirit that Paul lists in Galatians:

> But the fruit of the Spirit is love, joy, peace, longsuffering, kindness, goodness, faithfulness, gentleness, and self-control. Against such there is no law. And those *who are* Christ's have crucified the flesh with its passions and desires. If we live in the Spirit, let us also walk in the Spirit.[50]

This notion of "walking in the Spirit" is not a fairy tale nor a fantasy, but a reality in which Paul lived. It's a mode of being filled with the fruit of the Spirit and came as a result of yoking himself to Jesus and learning from him. We can step into that realm as well, if we will only take the path that he took.

These concrete areas of spiritual fruitfulness are where we find what the Celtic Christians called "thin places."[51] They believed that there were places, holy places, here on earth where the distance between heaven and earth is paper thin. There they would build shrines, churches, and

---

[50] Galatians 5:22-25

[51] Tracey Balzer, *Thin Places: An Evangelical Journey into Celtic Spirituality*, (Abilene Christian University Press, 2007).

monasteries so that the faithful could recognize them and take advantage to pray. Even though I must admit there have been geographical locations that made me feel closer to heaven, I wouldn't go so far as to say physical thin places exist.

Even so, I can tell you that by taking these on-ramps, I have consistently found myself led to the places where my soul seems more attuned to and focused on eternity. These are places of greater confidence, increased humility, true peace, uncomfortable yet necessary vulnerability, serious self-control, real compassion, jaw-dropping awe, and deeper wholeness. I have realized "an order is no burden when it is given by one who helps in carrying it out. To what place are we to follow Christ if not where he has already gone?"[52] It is as though, for us, the famous prayer commonly accredited to Jonathan Edwards that God would "stamp eternity on [his] eyeballs" has come to pass. It has not led to a physical destination, but to a nevertheless real destination.

---

[52] Thomas C. Oden, Christopher A. Hall, *Ancient Christian Commentary on Scripture: Mark*, (InterVarsity Press, 2014), 107.

It's a stretch

WE'LL GO A LONG WAY in clarifying the mysterious nature of paradox by deferring to one of our modern cultural commentators, Forrest Gump. The Tom Hanks character in one of the more profound moments in the film explained this idea living with paradox with such simplicity when he said, "I don't know if we each have a destiny, or if we're all just floatin' around accidental-like on a breeze, but I, I think maybe it's both. Maybe both is happenin' at the same time."[53]

That is a brilliant summary of what I am attempting to explain. The tension created in our lives can result in a stretching that can be viewed as a pain to our warped nature, but it is always pain with purpose. The yoke of Jesus will pull us in different directions, but with the sole purpose of making sure we are pointed in the right direction, always moving ever closer to him.

This tension caused by accepting both/and answers serves us in many ways that have nothing to do with our carnal nature. I have found that in some unusual way this tension also stretches me and, by keeping me pliable, makes space for grace. I can see it in Jesus' teaching in Luke 5. When you read, notice the paradox throughout the lesson:

---

[53] Robert Zemeckis, *Forrest Gump,* Paramount Pictures, 1994

> They said to him, "John's disciples often fast and pray, and so do the disciples of the Pharisees, but yours go on eating and drinking." Jesus answered, "Can you make the friends of the bridegroom fast while he is with them? But the time will come when the bridegroom will be taken from them; in those days they will fast." He told them this parable: "No one tears a piece out of a new garment to patch an old one. Otherwise, they will have torn the new garment, and the patch from the new will not match the old. And no one pours new wine into old wineskins. Otherwise, the new wine will burst the skins; the wine will run out and the wineskins will be ruined. No, new wine must be poured into new wineskins. And no one after drinking old wine wants the new, for they say, 'The old is better.'"[54]

Were they supposed to fast and pray or were they supposed to eat and drink? Jesus in essence replied, "Yes." There is a time for both.

This created tension because his disciples, like us, struggled with his both/and answers. They wanted to know exactly which was most important. We must live in this place of tension caused by paradoxical imperatives if we are to live an exponential life. The tension created by this teaching is compared to a wineskin that must be flexible,

[54] Luke 5:36-39, NIV

stretched, and pliable so that it can contain all that is poured into it. I, too, need this tension in my life to remain pliable and stretched so that I have an ever-increasing space to receive the vast quantities of grace and divine guidance my master is pouring out.

On-ramps create the tension

WHEN WE READ the New Testament as a whole — the Acts of the Apostles, the apostolic epistles, and especially the life of Jesus in the Gospels — we see clear signs of these paradoxical imperatives that we are to follow to create the needed tension in our spiritual lives on our route to the exponential life. Some on-ramps, while equally necessary, may appear contradictory. In prayer, our asking is as vital as our need to listen. Our pilgrimage into the wilderness is no less pivotal than our residence in our community. There is a clear tension that must be maintained between denying yourself and healing yourself through Sabbath. The tension lies within the long holding of true worship and adoration coupled with the required releasing of radical generosity. When we fully embrace the paradox of Jesus' imperatives, they create the "tension of opposites."

Morrie Schwartz described this phenomenon before his death in *Tuesdays with Morrie*:

> Life is a series of pulls back and forth. You want to do one thing, but you are bound to do something else. Something hurts you, yet you know it shouldn't. You take certain things for granted, even when you know you should never take anything for granted. A tension of opposites, like a pull on a rubber band. And most of us live somewhere in the middle."[55]

While it might be frightening at first, we were created to be stretched between the pulling of the paradoxes.

So few of us ever find this sweet spot between the two worlds laid out by Jesus for his followers. Most of us are prone to take the path of least resistance in almost every aspect of our lives. Our spiritual life is no exception. Psychologist Carl Jung was right when he said, "The greater the tension, the greater is the potential."[56] We can only go as far in the exponential life as we are willing to be stretched, and no more. I must admit that being stretched can be a tiring and lonely reality, yet living without the intended tension is even more exhausting.

Visualize it like this: You anchor yourself to one side by committing to follow Jesus' example and teachings concerning a specific on-ramp. Tension is created when you make

---

[55] Mitch Albom, *Tuesdays with Morrie*, (Warner Paperback, 2000), 40.

[56] Carl Jung, Collected Works of C.G. Jung: Alchemical Studies Volume 13, (Taylor & Francis, UK, 2014, 118.

an effort as a result of obedience to move toward another paradoxical on-ramp in the opposite direction. All of this is in the service of adopting the yoke of Jesus. It's not unlike stringing a bow. Those who refuse to live in this tension will be like a person who has a rope and sled that needs to be moved. Pushing on the rope may be easy and successfully avoids tension, but it will prove equally fruitless and frustrating.

There is no sense in pushing what was meant to be pulled simply because it is easier. Before long those who do so will confess through their sweat and dismay that their plan isn't working out so well. Jung reminds us that in life, "there is no energy unless there is a tension of opposites."[57] Without this energy, created by tension, a relationship with Jesus becomes a chore, a weight, or a frustration. The refusal of this tension and the resulting exasperation is the main reason people walk away from the faith. As Christian apologist G. K. Chesterton saw, "The Christian ideal has not been tried and found wanting; it has been found difficult and left untried."[58]

The tension that the paradoxical imperatives generate is there to make us the truly faithful Christ followers we were created to be. Jesus intends for these on-ramps to serve dual

---

[57] Jung, Carl . Two Essays on Analytical Psychology. United Kingdom, Routledge, 1992, 53

[58] G.K. Chesterton, *What's Wrong with the World*, (1910), part I, Chapter 5.

purposes. The teachings of Jesus are paradoxical to the upside-down world in which we live. This becomes more apparent with every passing day. Jesus knew that for us to become who he had created us to be, it would be necessary for us to become paradoxical, and only then would we reach our goal. One on-ramp counters the background noise and yelling of our culture, our times, and our society. Another counters our humanity, our hidden enemies that come disguised as productivity and busyness, and all of our dangerous selves that vie for attention and affections.

Supernatural slingshots and serendipitous shakings

IN ACTS 1, on the eve of the Ascension of Jesus, we see a dynamic facet of the Holy Spirit's work. In verse 8, when Jesus offered some closing words to his disciples, we receive a fuller glimpse of what is truly promised to us. The disciples were in the midst of asking 1,001 questions about what would happen next when Jesus assured them that they would "receive power when the Holy Spirit has come upon you and you shall be witnesses to Me in Jerusalem, and in all Judea and Samaria, and to the end of the earth."[59] Then, he immediately exited earth, stage left. He departed, prom-

[59] Acts 1:8

ising them nothing more than the hope of a second work of grace in the form of a dynamic power that would allow them to do things they never dreamed of doing. This power allowed them to become so fruitful in their spiritual life that their sons and daughters, grandkids, and even their great-great-great-great grandkids, all the way up to the present day and including us, would all still be in awe of what their lives produced.

This power is far from being about feelings and goosebumps. We can see the pivot point in the middle of that statement after the promise of the power followed by the word *and*. The promise was for a dynamic power that would serve to produce fruit in our lives. This power did indeed come through for the disciples and the same is on the table for each of us. Because of this power we seek to truly worship God and in doing so find the experience occurs naturally. Those awestruck supernatural moments are a fixed part of this landscape, and are part and parcel of the exponential life.

This comes to pass for many reasons, but there are two in particular I want to emphasize. The first is the "supernatural slingshot effect." It is when we are living in the tension created between the paradoxical imperatives. As a result of the stretching, we experience a moment, a situation, or a season of our life that has such gravitas that it pulls us along at a speed we could never have achieved on our own. Consider the harrowing journey of Apollo 13. When the craft was compromised, the only way to return to earth was to slingshot themselves around the moon.[60] We are simply borrowing gravity from something larger than ourselves to arrive at a level unreachable before. It's a form of spiritual drafting behind a larger object that allows us to move faster toward our goals because we are being shielded from the drag of the wind.

We can see a glimpse of the slingshot effect in Paul's lovely prayer for his readers in Ephesians 3:14-19:

> For this reason I bow my knees to the Father of our Lord Jesus Christ, from whom the whole family in heaven and earth is named, that He would grant you, according to the riches of His glory, to be strengthened with might through His Spirit in the inner man, that Christ may dwell in your hearts through faith; that you, being rooted and grounded in love, may be able to comprehend with all the saints what is the width and length and depth and height — to know the love of Christ which passes knowledge; that you may be filled with all the fullness of God.
>
> Now to Him who is able to do exceedingly abundantly above all that we ask or think, according to the power that works in us, to Him be glory in the church by Christ Jesus to all generations, forever and ever. Amen.

---

[60] https://sservi.nasa.gov/articles/apollo-13-commander-remembers-the-aborted-moon-mission/

Remember the power that works in us is none other than the Holy Spirit. I pray that we, too, will see our journeys on these paradoxical on-ramps in the following chapters as intended to be seen — as an impetus for the increased work of the Holy Spirit in our lives, leading us above and beyond in our pursuit of a fruitful spiritual life.

Another common supernatural occurrence is the shaking of the Holy Spirit. These events are just as productive as the aforementioned slingshots. These are not just any shakings, but what I have found to be "serendipitous shakings." There will come times of great growth in our spiritual lives as we submit to the tension. Some of those times are sunny and victorious, while others are filled with clouds and rain. These moments of shaking can come when we least expect it and are not of our choosing, much like the great storm that hit England on Oct. 16, 1987. It left a path of destruction across the country and destroyed tens of millions of cherished trees in the land, including the Turner Oak that had been planted in Kew Gardens in the 1700s. The centerpiece of the entire botanical garden, it was uprooted, shaken by the winds, then set back into its spot.

The gardeners were distraught to think that this lovely landmark would be no more. To make matters worse, they found it completely rotten in the middle. This new discovery took even more wind from their sails, convincing them the tree faced a quick demise. Because it was the most beloved tree in the park and one of the most well known in the entire country, the caretakers decided to make it the last of the destroyed trees to be cut up into pieces for removal. Due to the massive amount of fallen trees, it took three years to get to the Turner Oak.[61] When the time came, a close inspection revealed the tree had serendipitously shaken back into place. The tree had been saved by loosening its overly packed root base and allowing a much-needed breath of restoration.

The Turner Oak not only survived, it healed completely and it also has grown more in the last few decades than it had in all the previous centuries combined. Paul writes such an analogy in Romans 8:26-28:

> Likewise the Spirit also helps in our weaknesses. For we do not know what we should pray for as we ought, but the Spirit Himself makes intercession for us with groanings which cannot be uttered. Now He who searches the hearts knows what the mind of the Spirit is, because He makes intercession for the saints according to the will of God. And we know that all things work together for good to those who love God, to those who are the called according to His purpose.

---

[61] BBC Witness History Program, *The oak tree in Kew Gardens that taught the world a lesson* (Run January 29, 2020).

During these times of shaking — when we feel that everything is coming apart — if we are truly living to become fruitful, we can be certain that rather than destroying us, it may in fact bring us life. The same moments that break our hearts can, through the work of the Holy Spirit, refresh our souls.

During this time, the Holy Spirit's deepest work will take place. It will bring us to the place where we will grow like never before, and we can profess as Paul did, "We know that all things work together for good to those who love God, to those who are the called according to His purpose." This life that occurs between faith and works produces the supernatural slingshots and serendipitous shakings. It is the place where we grow to understand as followers of Christ what the readers of Ephesians 3 knew: God is indeed "able to do exceedingly abundantly above all that we ask or think, according to the power that works in us."[62]

Places of consistent and intense obedience can bring dead things to life, much like Abba John of the Desert, who obediently watered a dead and shriveled branch at the command of his spiritual father. Over time what to all appearances was a hopelessly dried up shell of its former self, sprouted back to life and produced fruit, the "fruit of

62 Ephesians 3:20-21

obedience."[63] This same coming alive allows us to become true worshippers of God, no matter how dead we may be.

Reality check

The tension created in our lives performs several functions. It creates supernatural power, it opens us up to receive more of what God is pouring out, it helps us to maintain balance, and it allows us to become more durable. It in no way functions to cause us harm. Over the course of church history, many have taken these on-ramps to their extremes, exacting great damage to themselves and others. It has been my disappointing experience that many Christians are simply looking for a new worksheet on which they can dutifully check the boxes, get a ribbon of completion, and move on to the next new thing. Others are in it for rewards and recognition. We must remember that Jesus never intended these paradoxical on-ramps to become anything more than a means to an end.

Anthony of the Desert knew this when he taught a young Egyptian hunter a lesson about the tension caused by the paradoxical life:

---

[63] His story is found in the book by Michael Elgamal, *A Forest in the Desert: The life of St. John the Short*, (Creative Orthodox, 2019).

> A hunter happened to come by and saw Anthony talking in a relaxed way with the brothers, and he was shocked. The hermit wanted to show him how he should sometimes be less austere for the sake of the brothers, and said to him, "Put an arrow in your bow, and draw it." He did so, and Anthony said, "Draw it further," and he drew it further. He said again, "Draw it further," and he drew it some more. Then the hunter said to him, "If I draw it too far, the bow will snap." Anthony answered, "So it is with God's work. If we always go to excess, the brothers quickly become exhausted. It is sometimes best not to be rigid."[64]

God wants to put tension in our lives for the purpose of making room in our warped nature for the exponential life, but he does not do it to damage us. For that reason, it is important to constantly allow yourself to be pulled back onto the opposite on-ramp to make sure your tension is not becoming too rigid or unbearable, and therefore damaging.

In this journey we are all beginners, even after decades of trudging forward, yoked to Jesus. Some may not like the title, which is understandable, but in this endeavor of becoming exponentially alive "let us be convinced of the fact that we will never be anything else but beginners."[65]

---

[64] Abba Anthony Curley, *The Thirty Eight Sayings of Saint Anthony*, (CreateSpace, 2017), 58.

[65] Thomas Merton, *Contemplative Prayer*, (Image Books, 1971), 13.

Make it personal

1. What places do you frequent when you are seeking the presence of God?

2. Which of the teachings of Jesus or the Bible seem paradoxical in nature to you?

3. Think back to a difficult season of your life. In what ways, if any, did it shape your character for the better?

Paradoxical Imperatives for Relating to God

4. On-Ramp of Listening

AS A CHILD, I spent endless summer days at Nanny's house with my cousins. She would always remind us, "God gave you two ears and one mouth. So you need to listen twice as much as you talk." Now, as a father of four, with the privilege of passing those same endless days with my own children cooped up in an ever-shrinking house, I know why she said it. But I didn't understand then that my grandmother was a philosopher at heart.

I could say that listening is a lost art, but that would mean at some time in human history it may have been found and mastered. If our current situation reveals anything, it is that it has never been found. My grandmother's aphorism was coined over 2,400 years ago by the Greek philosopher Diogenes. It reflects the innate human desire to be heard. As author Stephen Covey confessed, "Most people do not listen with the intent to understand; they listen with the intent to reply."[66]

It seems in our modern world listening takes a bit more effort. Have you ever carried on a conversation with a kid playing a video game? Or maybe attempted to talk with your spouse as he or she texted someone else? We get bits

---

[66] Stephen Covey, *Seven Habits of Highly Effective People: Powerful Lessons in Personal Change*, (Free Press, 2004), 239.

and pieces of what is being said because we are unwilling to pump the brakes long enough to listen. The same was true in Jesus' day. Everyone would come out to see the traveling miracle sideshow and no one wanted to slow down long enough to listen to what he really said. Even before the advent of electronics, we learned "you cannot truly listen to anyone and do anything else at the same time."[67] That includes our attempts to marvel at supernatural works of grace.

In Luke 6:46, Jesus proclaimed in frustration, "But why do you call Me 'Lord, Lord,' and not do the things which I say?" They came for the bread, for the show, for the supernatural, but they never stopped long enough to listen to the heart of his message that offered them a different way of life. In Mark 7, he healed the deaf man and allowed him to hear again, yet he could not change the Pharisees because they had chosen to ignore him and consequently became deaf to the Spirit. Just look at the number of times Jesus proclaimed to his followers, "He who has ears, let him hear." It was not enough to simply "have ears." It took a conscious effort to listen to what he said.

The lavish script found in Hebrews not only confirms this message, but if considered carefully, it screams at the top of its lungs. First in chapter 3 and then in chapter 4 we

---

[67] M. Scott Peck, *The Road Less Traveled: A New Psychology of Love, Traditional Values and Spiritual Growth*, (Simon & Schuster, 1974), 125.

hear the pleading to "please listen, don't turn a deaf ear."[68] The tone of the writing reflects the worried parent of a stubborn teenager begging to be heard. The next chapter adds teeth to the supplication:

> I have a lot more to say about this, but it is hard to get it across to you since you've picked up this bad habit of not listening. By this time you ought to be teachers yourselves, yet here I find you need someone to sit down with you and go over the basics on God again, starting from square one — baby's milk, when you should have been on solid food long ago! Milk is for beginners, inexperienced in God's ways; solid food is for the mature, who have some practice in telling right from wrong.[69]

This lack of listening is a form of slothfulness or laziness that dooms us to continue living in our parents' basement spiritually when we should be out on our own with ever-increasing freedom. Yet those who are "dull of hearing" are not deaf, but solely indifferent. They simply have no intention of doing what they are told.

It is plain to see this dullness on open display in the church when God's words, whether rote or spontaneous, are treated like part of a lesson from our ninth-grade

---

68 Hebrews 3:6-8, 12-14; 4:7, MSG
69 Hebrews 5:11-14, MSG

algebra teacher. It is received as information that will never be of use in the future, but something that must be retained only until the moment of the exam and then to be filed away under useless information in our subconscious. Compare this to the attentiveness afforded a cardiologist trying to explain a way of extending your time on earth after you had survived a heart attack. Those insights, rather than being ignored, would lead to a change in your way of living and a better quality of life. How much more should we commit ourselves to listening to God whose reach and understanding extends into eternity? It is clear that the author of Hebrews pointed us in the direction of this heightened level of listening, practically affixing our growth in spiritual maturity to it and showing that it begins and ends with our commitment to listen.

Posturing yourself to be a listener

SINCE IT'S AN ART we aren't born with, how do we learn to listen? First and foremost it requires humility. In high school, I walked out of my Spanish class because I had reached the conclusion that it would never serve me in what I thought my life's trajectory would be. I was determined to be an engineer and couldn't be bothered with something as petty as acquiring a new language. It wasn't until years later that I found myself living in a Spanish-speaking country, suffering daily humiliations as I attempted to communicate with locals. My level of Spanish hovered at the level of a 3-year-old child until I received the opportunity to learn at a linguistic institute in Costa Rica. I was finally ready to listen.

I had reached the level of wisdom of positively knowing what I did not know. I did not know all the answers and I needed help. This shift in my posture changed everything. I went from a headstrong person who did not want to listen to a gracious sponge who absorbed even the smallest detail. Humility is key. It can be sought out and applied in your life or it can come, as in my case, from humiliation and failure. Either way you choose to allow it to flow into your life, you will need large doses of it if you are truly going to live the exponential life.

This humility allows us to admit that the assumptions we have about life are most likely wrong and need to be corrected by Jesus' message. Our desire to listen and learn becomes greater than our desire for being right or our readiness in being offended. This admission opens us up and makes us vulnerable to the gospel. It shines a light into the depths of our being and illuminates even the hidden corners of our life. We are not, nor will we ever become, know-it-all disciples. At times our pride causes us to tune out the Holy Spirit and chart our own preferred course no matter how warped it may be.

Augustine noted this when considering the importance of taking on the yoke of Jesus:

> You are to "take my yoke upon you, and learn from me." You are not learning from me how to refashion the fabric of the world, nor to create all things visible and invisible, nor to work miracles and raise the dead. Rather, you are simply learning of me: "that I am meek and lowly in heart."[70]

We do this with confidence, that by following Jesus' lead, we will inherit the earth.[71]

Next is to realize the power of the thoughts you allow to penetrate your subconscious. What you listen to is in fact forming what you think. It is the admission that your thoughts are controlled by the images and the ideas that fill your subconscious.[72] Our minds become battlefields for

---

[70] Manlio Simonetti, *Ancient Christian Commentary on Scripture: Matthew 1-13*, (InterVarsity Press, 2014), Matthew 11:28-29.

[71] Psalm 37:11, Matthew 5:5

[72] Original Quote, "This may be a bit more than many people could find credible for this life, but it is clearly the direction in which we can and should be moving as apprentices of Jesus. What we surely can say is that those who are dead to self are not controlled in thought, feeling, or action by self-exaltation or by the will to have their own way, but are easily controlled by love of God and neighbor. They still have some sensitivity to self-will, no doubt, and are never totally beyond the possibility of falling under subjugation to it. Only a proper discipline and grace will prevent this from actually happening. But they no longer

competing ideological forces. As Paul wrote in 2 Corinthians 10:3-6:

> For though we walk in the flesh, we do not war according to the flesh. For the weapons of our warfare are not carnal but mighty in God for pulling down strongholds, casting down arguments and every high thing that exalts itself against the knowledge of God, bringing every thought into captivity to the obedience of Christ, and being ready to punish all disobedience when your obedience is fulfilled.

The enemy of our soul and our very own subversive, warped selves are doing everything to undermine our journey toward an exponential life.

This realization puts us on a different footing. Jesus expounds more on this idea in Mark 7:20-23,

> What comes out of a man, that defiles a man. For from within, out of the heart of men, proceed evil thoughts, adulteries, fornications, murders, thefts, covetousness, wickedness, deceit, lewdness, an evil eye, blasphemy, pride, foolishness. All these evil things come from within and defile a man.

---

are locked in a struggle with it." Dallas Willard, *Renovation of the Heart*, (NavPress, 2002), 142.

We must take seriously our need to listen intently to God and his eternal truth, rather than the noisy gods of this present age.

The believer who refuses to admit this ongoing war for their thoughts is like a river I crossed many times while serving as a missionary in the Amazon jungle. This particular point of land is a place of stunning natural beauty, the walls of the canyon rise well over the height of a 10-story building on all sides, and it is covered in lush vegetation. At the bottom of the canyon there is a confluence of two rivers. Here, dark muddy water merges with crystal clear mountain water. The two remain separate until the muddy and warmer jungle water fully changes the temperature of the cold mountain water. But little by little the mud takes over. So it is with our minds.

Many times I have realized too late that I spend too much time focusing on the wrong information. Listening to 24-hour news, social media, and even other misinformed Christians can slowly but surely begin to reshape our thoughts. We must be willing to take hold of every interaction and to ask each of the following questions. Is this ascending from my carnal nature or descending from heaven? Is this a reflection of God as revealed in the Incarnation? Is this a temporary issue that is part of the shifting-sand landscape of our popular culture? Is it a lie from the father of lies?

Finally, I must be willing to trust in the goodness of God and obey what we have heard from him. As we begin to listen to God and take the on-ramps Jesus identified that lead us to the exponential life we will inevitably reach a place of great discomfort. It will eventually cause us to confront our ideas of comfort and happiness. We will be faced with tough decisions. At times we will think we misunderstood God or we will linger at a tough scriptural text awaiting the asterisk to appear that exonerates us from obedience. This desire of wanting what we want instead of what God wants for us has always been and always will be a stumbling block to real listening.

Of Jesus' warnings on the danger of drunken behavior in Luke 21, English monk the Venerable Bede wrote:

> Suppose a physician should bid us beware of the juice of a certain herb, lest a sudden death overtake us, we should most earnestly attend to his command: but when our Savior warns us to shun drunkenness and surfeiting, and the cares of this world, men have no fear of being wounded and destroyed by them; for the faith with they put in the caution of the physicians, they disdain to give to the words of God.[73]

[73] Venerable Bede, *Catena Aurea :Commentary on the Four Gospels, Out of the Works of the Fathers,* (1861), Luke 21:34-36.

This statement is both ancient and true. We look to others and experts on life and ignore the words of the actual Creator because they make us a little uncomfortable, don't make sense to us, or ask us to give up something we really want to possess. Our goal in listening is not simply gaining information, nor understanding, but transformation. When we listen to God, we are allowing him to point out "the plank in our own eye"[74] that may be causing us to not see situations as clearly as we should. Yet those who choose to be blind to the instruction of the Lord don't listen because they are afraid of what God is trying to tell them.

Jesus said that his sheep will know his voice.[75] But in a world filled with noise, how does a disciple know his voice? Even before children have the full capacity of eyesight, they can recognize the voice of their parents. It is the result of frequency, formed by continual listening. In fact, our commitment to listening attentively is the first step in shortening the response time we have between our hearing and doing. We must understand that our delay is damaging to us. As Thomas à Kempis found out, "Instant obedience is the only kind of obedience there is; delayed obedience is disobedience. Whoever strives to withdraw from obedience, withdraws from Grace."[76]

---

[74] Matthew 7:3-5

[75] John 10:2, 27

[76] This is my modernization of the original quote found by Thomas à Kempis, *Thomas à Kempis Collection*, (Rivingtons, UK, 1887), 91.

Who doesn't love Jeremiah 29:11? We write it in calligraphy and frame it for gifts. It warms our heart and fills us with hope. The prophet's assurance, "I know the plans I have for you..."[77] is a great comfort in an ever-more uncertain world. But what it doesn't say is, "I'm going to do it the easiest, simplest, most comfortable way or in the way that will make you happiest." God has an exponential plan for your life, but he will not always do it the way you think it should be done. For that reason, you must ready yourself to obey what you hear, even when it doesn't make sense or it makes you uncomfortable.

Is it really reading if no one is listening?

I REMEMBER THE MOMENT the statement changed my life. I was serving my first term as a missionary in South America and I found myself in an adult Sunday School class. Spanish was a struggle. Each phrase had to be grasped and fully interpreted for me to make heads or tails out of it. My supervising missionary asked a question concerning our church's commitment to daily Bible reading. "I don't want to know if you read your Bible," he said. "I want to know if you listened."

---

[77] NIV

It fell on fertile soil, took root quickly, and began to bear fruit almost immediately. It solved my conundrum of feeling like I was in a valley and that God no longer reached out to me. In that moment my daily drudgery of reading a few chapters and running out the door was transformed completely. I realized that I had never allowed myself to engage the text or to be engaged by the Word of God.

I had been to Bible school. I was taught the importance of reading the Bible from the moment of my conversion. My problem was the same as the one 20th century missionary Frank Laubach described: "The trouble with nearly everybody who prays is that he says 'Amen' and runs away before God has a chance to reply. Listening to God is far more important than giving Him our ideas."[78] I had even delved into the monastic practice *Lectio Divina,* or Divine Reading, in my pursuit of a deeper, more contemplative daily devotion. I constantly found that I was simply checking the box for the daily task of flipping a few pages, never pausing to allow the Holy Spirit to speak to me.

As I attempted to run through the list, I would drift into a swamp of worthless preoccupation that eventually rushed me out the door without ever allowing the Living Word to do its work. *Lectio Divina* is an amazing and proven spiritual discipline that I encourage you to explore more deeply. But

---

[78] Quote found in a pamphlet written by Frank Laubach entitled, "*The Game of Minutes,*" printed in 1951.

for me it had been nothing but a musty phrase. It made me think of monks writing, hunched over in candlelight, scribbling in Latin and Greek with quills and ink on sheepskin books while eating cheese and drinking stout wine. It seemed out of touch with my reality. I had no problem reading. I loved to read, but I struggled with listening. I had been trained to teach and preach the Bible, but I was running so furiously to do the work of God that I missed the God of the work.

I desperately needed to change my approach to the Word of God. One of the things that helped me was the realization that the vast majority of the Church throughout history did not have access to a written Bible. Our printed, ordered text is a Western novelty for those of us who have the honor of living in our current time and place. Early Christians depended on someone else to read the Bible for them. This places a premium on listening intently. It emphasizes listening to learn, listening to be taught, and listening to be transformed.

As a pastor and church leader, I have learned well from cable TV talk show host Larry King, who made a career of asking tough questions of some of the world's most important people. He divulged his secret: "I remind myself every morning: Nothing I say this day will teach me anything. So if I'm going to learn, I must do it by listening."[79]

[79] Larry King quote taken from a newsweek.com article, "The Best Quotes by Larry King" by Benjamin Fearnow.

What if we approached God this way? When we admit that listening is the first step on the way to an exponential life, it changes everything.

Over the past 20 years, I have made a daily practice of approaching the Word of God in an attitude of divine listening or *Auscultatio Divina.* The Latin phrase was even chosen by Benedict of Nursia to guide his students from among several options. He wanted to be sure he expressed his desire to "listen with an obedient ear" when he began his rule with the admonition to "Listen carefully my son, to the master's instructions and attend to them with the ears of your heart."[80] This "attentive listening of the heart" is much more "precise and profound" than simply hearing or reading.[81] *Auscultatio* has evolved into the modern word *auscultation,* which was formed in 1821 to describe what a doctor does when using a stethoscope to listen for internal organs, specifically the heart.

This practice of divine listening can be seen as listening to the heartbeat of God. We don't read the Bible to find answers to all of our questions; we read it to find Jesus and to hear his words directly. Granted, when we find Jesus as he is revealed in the Bible, we realize that he is the answer to all of our questions. It is an effort to obey our Heavenly Father's proclamation to all who would be Jesus' disciples

---

80 Noel O Sullivan, *Christ and Creation:Christology as the Key to Interpreting the Theology of Creation in the Works of Henri de Lubac,* (Peter Lang), 117.

81 Ibid

on the Mount of Transfiguration. From the tabernacle of the cloud, he boomed, "This is my beloved Son, with whom I am well pleased; listen to him."[82]

This practice of divine listening must be seen as more than hearing. It is a true indicator of a disciple of Christ. Leo of Rome gave special attention to the imperative:

> A voice from the cloud said, This is my beloved Son, with whom I am well pleased; listen to him. I am manifested through his preaching. I am glorified through his humility. So listen to him without hesitation. He is the truth and the life. He is my strength and wisdom. "Listen to him" whom the mysteries of the law foreshadowed, of whom the mouths of the prophets sang. "Listen to him" who by his blood redeemed the world, who binds the devil and seizes his vessels, who breaks the debt of sin and the bondage of iniquity. "Listen to him" who opens the way to heaven and by the pain of the cross prepares for you the steps of ascent into his kingdom. [83]

Read as a disciple instead of as a consumer. Listen to him. Read with the expectation to be inspired, guided, directed,

---

[82] Matthew 17:5

[83] Manlio Simonetti, *Ancient Christian Commentary on Scripture: Matthew 14-28*, (InterVarsity Press, 2014), 56.

and even corrected. Listen to him. Allow his Word to speak to your situation, your subconscious self, and your soul. Listen to him.

This way of listening changed the way I viewed the Bible. It changed the way I looked at nature. It changed the way I responded to prophetic words from trusted sources. It changed the way I sat in a church service. It became a balm of sorts that can heal and make whole. But just like the topical medicines of my childhood, it can also sting as Methodius of Olympus noted when he explained, "Now the whole spiritual meditation of the Scriptures is given to us as salt which stings in order to benefit. Without this disinfection, it is impossible for a soul, by means of reason, to be brought to the Almighty."[84] I have ultimately learned that the Bible is a book of eternal truth, given to build our faith, heal our souls, and confront our shortcomings. I do not want to miss its divine purpose because I fear the sting it may bring, and thus miss out on a fruitful life.

Listening has kept me on high alert and always leaning in to hear what God is saying to me. This discipline has bled into my other relationships and I have come to agree with martyred German theologian Dietrich Bonhoeffer who said, "Christians . . . so often think they must always contribute something when they are in the company of others, that this is the one service they have to render. They

---

[84] Thomas C. Oden, Christopher A. Hall, *Ancient Christian Commentary on Scripture: Mark*, (InterVarsity Press, 2014), 126.

forget that listening can be a greater service than speaking."[85] Learning to listen to God quickly became an asset to me as a minister of the gospel as it taught me to listen to others. Just as Eugene Peterson understood, "Speaking to people does not have the same personal intensity as listening to them. The question I put to myself is not 'How many people have you spoken to about Christ this week?' but 'How many people have you listened to in Christ this week?'"[86] Listening to God makes you more open to your neighbor.

This attentive listening for God's voice is found throughout our canon of Scripture. It is embodied in the prayer of the young boy Samuel when he cried out, "Speak, for your servant hears."[87] It is the heart cry found in the Old Testament Shema in Deuteronomy that Jesus repeated in Mark 12:29 that proclaims, "Hear oh Israel, the Lord our God, the Lord is One."[88] Jesus knew that above all else he would need to remind his disciples to "Hear" or "Listen up" if they were going to live the exponential life he had promised them.

When speaking to his disciples, Jesus promised we would not need to worry about what to say or how to say it, be-

---

[85] Ruth Haley Barton, *Life Together in Christ: Experiencing Transformation in Community*, (InterVarsity Press, 2014), 57.

[86] Eugene Peterson, *God's Message for Each Day: Wisdom from the Word of God*, (Thomas Nelson, 2020), 133.

[87] 1 Samuel 3:10.

[88] Deuteronomy 6:4

cause he would send us the Holy Spirit.[89] And as a result of Pentecost, the Comforter "will teach you all things and bring to your remembrance all things that I said to you."[90] Yet it leads me to question, how can Jesus teach us if we are unwilling to listen? If we are only sprinting through our devotional time to check the box and continue to live life as if God isn't speaking, what then? God is speaking constantly, but are you listening? To journey toward exponential life it is of utmost importance to realize as former agnostic Malcolm Muggeridge learned, "Everything happening, great and small, that is to say, is a parable whereby God speaks to us; and the art of life is to get the message."[91]

Listening to build spiritual storehouses

WHEN WE LIVE in faith and listen attentively to the Word of God, we can be sure that the Holy Spirit will come through in our daily lives. He will encourage us and allow us to encourage others, giving us the words we need, when we need them. I have found that the work of the Holy Spirit is even more potent when we have a spiritual store-

[89] Luke 12:11-12

[90] John 14:26

[91] Malcolm Muggeridge, *Christ and the Media,* (Regent College Publishing, Canada, 2003), 25.

house from which to draw. We know the team that Jesus formed when he called his disciples. They were not the top of their theology class, nor were they polished intellectuals. Yet over the course of time, as they listened to Jesus' teaching, they were transformed to the point that he considered them on par with the scribes and spiritual teachers of the day.

In Matthew 13 we see him summarizing his lesson by asking, "Have you understood all these things?" They said to Him, "Yes, Lord." They had practiced *Auscultatio Divina* and postured themselves daily to learn through humility, teachability, and expectation. And as a result, Jesus proclaimed to these roughneck fishermen, reformed tax collectors, and community rabble, "Therefore every scribe instructed concerning the kingdom of heaven is like a householder who brings out of his treasure [storehouse] things new and old."[92] That treasure or storehouse that Jesus refers to is the Word of God that we have hidden in our hearts. It is in the depths of our subconscious and as a result on the tip of our tongues.

How can we add to and draw from this storehouse? First, understand it requires consistency and should be attended to daily, just as with your other appointments and tasks. If you make the time to listen, you can be assured that God will be speaking. Bring a notebook and pen in an-

[92] Matthew 13:51-52

ticipation that you will need to write down what you read or what is impressed on your heart while you read. Have a set plan to follow. There are several places to start, but if you have never attempted it, begin with the New Testament and read a chapter a day.

As you read, ask questions of the portion you are reading. As English statesman Francis Bacon stated, "The right question is the halfway point to wisdom."[93] Don't waste your questions on frivolous things that don't change the narrative of what you are reading. Here are a few I ask often: What did God communicate to this audience? Why did he say it that particular way? What is the Holy Spirit saying to me through this text? Is this literal or a figure of speech? Does this reflect what I know about God? Does this contradict what I know about God? I encourage you to find a good study Bible, a good set of commentaries, and a Bible dictionary.

Don't forget to use the intellect that God has given you. As Bible scholar Gordon Fee stated:

> The concern of the scholar is primarily with what the text meant; the concern of the layperson is usually with what it means. The believing scholar insists that we must

---

[93]Updated quote from the original quote, "A prudent question is one-half of wisdom." Christy, Robert, *Proverbs Maxims and Phrases of all ages*, (G.P. Putnam's Sons, New York and London, The Knickerbocker Press, 1888) 184.

> have both. Reading the Bible with an eye only to its meaning for us can lead to a great deal of nonsense as well as to every imaginable kind of error — because it lacks controls. Fortunately, most believers are blessed with at least a measure of that most important of all hermeneutical skills — common sense.[94]

Your common sense will take you far in your listening.

Reading Scripture in this way and allowing God's Word to be personalized in our lives is explained by Jean-Pierre de Caussade, who encouraged his readers to, "Come, not to study the history of God's divine action, but to be its object; not to learn what it has achieved through the centuries and still does, but simply to be the subject of its operation."[95] There are also the more personal questions we may have about our reality. Contrary to the teachings of some misguided leaders, our life's circumstances are predominantly out of our control. In all likelihood, there are three types of people in the church: those who are currently in a trying time; those who are coming out of a trying time; or those who are about to go into a trying time. These times can serve as a wrecking ball in the battle for our thoughts,

---

[94] Gordon Fee, *How to Read the Bible for all its Worth*, (Zondervan, 2009), Preface.

[95] Paul Murray OP, *In the Grip of Light: The Dark and Bright Journey of Christian Contemplation*, (Bloomsbury Publishing, 2012), 11.

and we must learn to counter them with productive questions and thought patterns.

Commonly we ask the unproductive question, "Why is this happening to me?" Even if God appeared to me and said, "Joil, these are all the reasons why..." that answer does nothing to change my reality. It doesn't pay my rent if I have lost my job. It doesn't bring back my loved one who has died. It doesn't offer me joy when I am down. Yet if I bring the question, "What is God trying to do here?" into my time of sacred thinking, then, when the answer arrives, it cannot help but to effect change in me by altering my perspective and understanding. With that in hand, there is a possibility that I may be allowed to change the reality I am facing. Finally, it is so important to ask yourself one final question before closing your notebook: "What am I going to do about what God has said to me?"

But what about the times God says things that are just over our head or out of our comprehension? That does and will happen no matter your level of learning. Jesus clearly pointed out that the Pharisees in John 8 didn't understand his words because of their sinfulness. It wasn't that they *could not*. They had become obstinate and simply *would not*, all due to the reality of what he said. If what he said was true, then it condemned their way of life. As Richard Foster noted, that sin causes us to become "nearsighted and develop thickened eardrums." And as a result it leads us to an eventual "inability to discern the heart of God and an asking that is askew."[96] Is there sin that is causing you to be deaf to what God is saying? Are you allowing your wants and wishes to override his eternal truths?

Other times when we cannot understand, it is because God is wanting you to lean into the text and listen more carefully. Early Church father John Chrysostom theorized that Jesus did this because, "he desires first to make them more attentive through their uncertainty, and by dark [hard] sayings like these to accustom them to listen to his words."[97] He is not trying to hide himself. He is trying to draw you deeper. But what if there are teachings we just never understand, no matter how long we listen?

Chrysostom again lets us know that we are not in any way wasting our time by attempting to understand God by attentive listening:

> If now we will thus search the Scriptures, exactly and not carelessly, we shall be able to attain unto our salvation; if we continually dwell upon them, we shall learn right doctrine and a perfect life. For although a man be very hard, and stubborn, and proud, and profit nothing at other times, yet at least he shall gain fruit from this

---

[96] Richard J. Foster, *Prayer: Finding the Heart's True Home*, (HarperSanFrancisco, 1992), 183-184.

[97] John Chrysostom, *The Complete Works of John Chrysostom: Cross linked to the Bible*, Philip Schaff Translation, (Kindle Version, 2016), John viii.20.

> time, and receive benefit, if not so great as to admit of his being sensible of it, still he shall receive it. For if a man who passes by an ointment-maker's shop, or sits in one, is impregnated with the perfume even against his will, much more is this the case with one who comes to church. For it cannot be that he who speaks with God, and hears God speak, should not profit.[98]

Make the decision to not rush on. Linger, willingly hold on to what you have heard and allow the Holy Spirit to draw you deeper. Allow yourself to keep the posture of a listener, because a listener is a learner. Commit to walk in obedience when you understand what God is saying, even if it is going to be difficult. Jesus notes in John 8:51, "If anyone keeps my words, he will never see death." Notice that this promise of the exponential life is not simply in the listening, but in the keeping that we find the promise.

Over the course of filling up your spiritual storehouse, you can expect the Holy Spirit to teach you, as well as bring to your remembrance what you have stored away.[99] Each day over the course of the past few years, I've spent time with Jesus and his teachings. As a result, I can hear his words coming to my mind as I go through my daily life. It has allowed me to see the world and its goings-on in a different light. It influences what I post on social media. It

---

[98] Ibid

[99] John 14:26

changes the way I treat my family, my friends, and especially my enemies. It has helped me to see life in the midst of a dead world. It gives me hope in hopeless situations. It is refreshing to be informed by eternal truth instead of simply being opinionated. We tend to look more like Jesus when we listen to God, instead of trying to make God's word fit to what we say.

When you have committed to this on-ramp of divine listening, your spiritual storehouse will begin to fill up. You will have the truest truth at the heart of your life. You will trade shifting sands for the bedrock of eternal truth. This does not make you rigid or cold, but fills you with confidence — not a prideful self-confidence, but a complete confidence in God. This assurance is reflected in the apostle Paul's words in 2 Timothy: "For this reason I also suffer these things; nevertheless I am not ashamed, for I know whom I have believed and am persuaded that He is able to keep what I have committed to Him until that Day."[100]

So picture yourself with a daily appointment, a set time and place where you will meet with God. You arrive with a Bible, a notebook, and a pencil in hand, ready to listen, learn, receive direction, and even correction on living the exponential life. You posture yourself with the expectation that something life-changing will be conveyed. It may be solely for you and, like the Virgin Mary, you will need to

---

[100] 2 Timothy 1:12

treasure it up in your heart and hold on to it for the right time. Alternatively, it may be something to encourage someone in need or in defense of your faith. Regardless of the circumstances, you can rely on the Holy Spirit to bring it out if you have stocked the shelves of your spiritual storehouse.

God is speaking. He has guidance and direction for you. It tends to be more with a nudge than a body slam, but the ultimate question is, are you listening? Are you open to whatever God may say? Are you in the moment or are you drifting on to another time and place? Are you listening and holding what God is saying or simply waiting your turn to talk?

Make it personal

1. Observe your upcoming conversations with care. Do you notice a difficulty in letting the person you're talking to finish? Have you meaningfully retained the content of what they've told you?

2. What has been your experience when you've made efforts to listen to God? What has been the experience of your close friends and family?

3. What is your instinct when you receive and understand a hard teaching from God or his Word?

4. What are the primary distractions that make listening a challenge for you?

5. On-Ramp of Prayer

AFTER THE DISCIPLES observed the many angles of Jesus' life — the preaching, the teaching, the miracles, the daily grind — they made a special request. It wasn't to learn about angels, demons, or the afterlife. It wasn't to find out his secrets in preaching or how to heal the sick. After several years of following his lead they had only one request: "Teach us to pray." They had seen his life, his ministry, and his works. They knew the secret behind his success in these areas. In Luke 11:5-10 he told them:

> Which of you shall have a friend, and go to him at midnight and say to him, "Friend, lend me three loaves; for a friend of mine has come to me on his journey, and I have nothing to set before him;" and he will answer from within and say, "Do not trouble me; the door is now shut, and my children are with me in bed; I cannot rise and give to you;" I say to you, though he will not rise and give to him because he is his friend, yet because of his persistence he will rise and give him as many as he needs. So I say to you, ask, and it will be given to you; seek, and you will find; knock, and it will be opened

> to you. For everyone who asks receives, and he who seeks finds, and to him who knocks it will be opened.

When reading this parable, we see the need to not only pray, but to persist in prayer.

This principle of patient and persistent asking runs counter to our culture, which is accustomed to leaving a bad review or a scathing hashtag post. Rather than being dismayed by our continued asking, let us understand as evangelist D. L. Moody did when he wrote, "Some people think God does not like to be troubled with our constant coming and asking. The way to trouble God is not to come at all."[101] The apostle Paul knew this when he told the Thessalonians that they should "pray without ceasing."[102] Rather than simply allowing our prayers to be a sanctified wish list, we must realize what educator William J. McGill explained: "The value of persistent prayer is not that God will hear us, but that we will finally hear God."[103] Again, it is about listening.

The goal of prayer is not primarily to change our circumstances, although that is one of its benefits. It is

---

[101] Sally Lloyd-Jones, *Thoughts to Make Your Heart Sing: Vol. 3*, (Zonderkids, 2012), 221.

[102] 1 Thessalonians 5:16-17

[103] Timothy M. Dolan, *Priest for the Third Millennium*, (Our Sunday Visitor, 2009) Chapter 6. Or https://www.xavier.edu/jesuitresource/online-resources/quote-archive1/quotes-about-prayer.

about submitting myself to what God is doing around me, in me, and through me. It is honestly battling through my doubts, so that I can accept God's will and what he is doing, no matter how painful it may be to me at the moment. At times it may seem we can only muster the prayer of the desperate father who looked at Jesus and confessed in Mark 9:23-25, "Lord, I believe; help my unbelief!" His prayer was not rejected. He was not lectured by Jesus. His request proved to be effective, simply because it was honest.

Prayer is also the confession of my complete reliance on God and my trust in his good plan, rather than my short-sighted goals and machinations. It is my frequent confession that I truly believe what Jesus said when he proclaimed, "Whoever abides in me and I in him, he it is that bears much fruit, for apart from me you can do nothing."[104] The reason to persist in prayer is our utter dependence on God. Augustine urged his followers to "Pray as though everything depended on God. Work as though everything depended on you."[105] C. S. Lewis, as depicted in the 1993 film *Shadowlands*, showed his dependence when he admitted, "I pray because I can't help myself. I pray because I'm helpless. I pray because the need flows out of me all the time,

[104] John 15:5, ESV

[105] Warren Wiersbe, *Bible Exposition Commentary, New Testament Volume 1,* (Victor Books, 2003) 419.

waking and sleeping. It doesn't change God. It changes me."[106]

For those of us who come from a non-liturgical church background, the greatest struggle in prayer can come from our belief that the only real prayer is the casual spontaneous prayer. This leads us to be self-centered, spur-of-the-moment, and more focused on fulfilling our wishes and wants instead of God's will. Somehow we believe that maybe Jesus missed it somewhere when he taught his disciples that they would, "pray then like this" and followed it with a formalized prayer that we call the Lord's Prayer.[107]

Many refuse to simply obey this teaching, thinking that they have a better way of doing it or that formality will somehow cause prayer to lose its power. Those "better ways" are much like bushwhacking while hiking. This attitude can lead us into some amazing, spontaneous places with astonishing views, but they can also lead us into frustration. Before we know it, we are staring at a wall counting the bricks, thinking about the score of the ballgame, or navel gazing because we lost our train of thought. It is true that "prayer is friendship with God." We all know that "friendship is not formal," but neither is it "formless."[108]

---

[106] Attenborough, Richard (director) (1993). *Shadowlands* [Film]. Price Entertainment.

[107] Matthew 6:9-13, Luke 11:1-4

[108] Richard Foster and James Bryan Smith, Devotional Classics, (Harper Collins, 2005), 87.

I agree with Dallas Willard when he suggests that many Christians never fully realize their potential in prayer because they refuse to follow the model prayer that Jesus laid out.[109] Many years ago I fell in love with the marked path of the Lord's Prayer. I became convinced that we can be sure that this path laid out by Jesus covers "all that we have need of, even before we ask."[110] When fully engaged, it can lead me to some of the greatest views available in the spiritual world and it will allow me to prevail over myself, so that I can choose to consume grace to become fruitful. I have come to agree with the ancients who described prayer as "a climbing up of the heart unto God."[111]

Structured daily prayers using the Psalter

ANY CHRISTIAN I have ever met knows that prayer is essential in the faith journey, yet it is constantly neglected and overlooked. It is simple to recognize the importance of prayer, but the commitment of time and effort needed to learn *how* to pray is where the sheep and the goats are separated. The goats will continually suffer from spiritual sick-

---

[109] Dallas Willard, *Divine Conspiracy*, (Harper, 1998) this thought is summarized from his exposition of the Lord's Prayer found on pages 253-269.

[110] Matthew 6:8

[111] Warren Wiersbe, *On Earth as it is in Heaven*, (Baker Publishing, 2010), 10.

ness because they refuse to keep company with God through prayer. Augustine of Hippo taught it this way:

> Remember this. When people choose to withdraw far from a fire, the fire continues to give warmth, but they grow cold. When people choose to withdraw far from light, the light continues to be bright in itself but they are in darkness. This is also the case when people withdraw from God.[112]

When we feel far from God or spiritually cold, it is not God who has stopped giving warmth. Instead, we have chosen to live in the cold because of our failure to keep company with the one in whose image we are made. This desire for true relational conversation is woven into our being. Gordon Fee said of our makeup, "God has made us this way, in his own image, because he himself is a personal, relational being."[113]

If we are made to relate to God, why do we still find it so challenging to pray? In my life it came down to two words: honesty and access. For some time, being genuine with God was a challenge. I struggled to speak my mind without fear of repercussions. I would skirt the issues and pray nice plas-

---

[112] Catherine Bernard and John Shea (editors), *Family: Heart of Humanity*, (Cambridge Scholars Publishing, UK, 2014), 23.

[113] Gordon Fee, *Paul, The Spirit, and The People of God*, (Hendrickson Publishers, 1996), 9.

tic prayers that I knew would be pleasing and not hurt God's feelings. It was misguided and unsustainable. All fake relationships are. We crave genuine relationships that allow us to let our hair down and speak without fear of judgment or hurt feelings. No one likes to keep company with a fragile ego and sadly for years that is exactly how I treated God. One way that I got real with God was by praying the Psalms.

The Book of Psalms is a prayer book and a hymn book, written by our godly ancestors and used in daily prayers by Jesus and his disciples. Chris Hall taught me, "The Psalms give us permission."[114] They allow us to be angry when things do not go the way we think they should (Psalm 13, 109); when people mistreat us (41, 55); when death knocks at our door (16, 116); when we fail and fall into sin (32, 51); when we are celebrating unforeseen victories (42, 139); when we feel like we cannot go on (23, 25, 91). Psalms articulate the spectrum of our emotions.

Bonhoeffer found that, "The more deeply we grow into the psalms and the more often we pray them as our own, the more simple and rich will our prayer become."[115] Inside the collection of 150 song prayers, we find the wonderful treasure of the Psalms of Ascents. These are from Psalm 120 through 134 and were written to be sung as prayers as

---

[114] Chris Hall quote from a talk given at the Renovaré Institute in Charlotte, North Carolina.

[115] Dietrich Bonhoeffer, *Life Together*, (HarperOne, 1978), 50.

the faithful prepared themselves to enter into God's Holy Temple. They are short and concise and deal with every raw emotion imaginable. As Eugene Peterson confessed during a video conversation with singer-songwriter Bono, Psalms allow us to "learn to cuss without cussing." As you journey toward the exponential life that Jesus promised, you need to allow yourself to become brutally honest in prayer, even when all you can muster is praying the prayer of the primal scream.

The next roadblock I had to overcome was realizing that by coming to God and getting real with him, I granted him the access I had been refusing him. My superficial prayers didn't open me up in a way for God to truly do his work in my life. Although I cannot hide my reality from God — he knows much better than I do what is really going on in my life and emotions — but in my pettiness, I try. I go through the dead motions and never truly open the door to allow him inside.

If a person is not careful, the same issue can surface in a marriage. I can usually tell when my wife is going through a difficult time, whether it's because of a staff problem at work leading a home for young at-risk girls, a concern about an upcoming change, or a hurt caused by someone close to her. At times I can even discern how to resolve the problem. But these realities matter very little if she will not grant me access to talk with her about it. It all depends on her desire to open up and get real with me.

The same goes for God. He knows everything, but he is waiting on us to grant him access. We give him that when we are honest in our prayer life. Our human nature has caused us to attempt to hide from him since the Garden of Eden. You can no more hide your reality behind your stiff prayers than our ancestors could using fig leaves. I can recall the first time I truly engaged the Psalms as a form of prayer. I found myself in a very difficult place, things were not moving the way I wanted them to, and I was angry, worried, and anxious. As I bowed my head and read out loud the opening stanza, "How long, oh Lord?" I broke. I wept. I opened myself up and got honest with God. I prayed and God came rushing into that moment.

Casting your cares and counting your blessings

ONE WAY OF GETTING REAL and granting access is what the apostle Peter pointed to when he admonished his readers, "Humble yourselves under the mighty hand of God, that He may exalt you in due time, casting all your care upon Him, for He cares for you."[116] Read that last line again: *...casting all your care upon Him.* Why? Because "he cares for you." True prayer has little to do with a grocery

[116] 1 Peter 5:7

list filled with your desires but it has everything to do with getting real with God. Soon after I made the decision to allow God to see the real me, I was astounded when I learned that, "As we pour out our bitterness, God pours in his peace."[117] When we grant access, we are allowing God to work as he sees fit in our situation. We are asking "thy will be done."[118]

This process opens us up to God's correction and intervention. We stop telling God what we think he should do and we reach a point of trusting that he will somehow glorify himself, no matter the situation. We learn to accept God's answer and know that it is good Alpha Course developer Nicky Gumbel expressed this idea well: "If God answers "yes," he is increasing your faith. If "wait," he is increasing your patience. If "no," he has something better for you."[119] We ultimately find that "prayer is aligning ourselves with the purposes of God."[120] Through this action of daily "casting our care" upon the Lord, we learn, as English preacher Charles Spurgeon did, to count "anything a bless-

---

[117] Doris Curtis, *Inspirational Thoughts to Warm the Soul: Quotations, Stories, and More*, (iUniverse, 2011), 270.

[118] Matthew 26:42

[119] Gumbel, N [@nicky Gumbel]. (2019, January 29). [Tweet]. Twitter. https://twitter.com/nickygumbel/status/1090339295980896256

[120] E Stanley Jones, *Beginning With Christ: Timeless Wisdom for Complicated Times*, (Abingdon Press, 2018), 205.

ing which makes us pray."[121] And for those who truly strive to "lay hold" of the exponential life Jesus has promised, you will recognize the blessing of God's "no" and "not now" answers. It doesn't require much hindsight to understand that many times God's greatest blessing has been to not respond immediately to our demands.

We must not overlook one of prayer's most important pur-poses: thanksgiving. The word has come to conjure thoughts of an autumnal turkey dinner, but the reality is that "we need deliberately to call to mind the joys of our journey."[122] It can be easy to forget that the apostle Paul points to it in almost half of his writings. 1 Thessalonians 5:16-18, Colossians 2:6-7, 15-17, Philippians 4:4-7, Ephesians 5:18-20, 2 Corinthians 9:15, and Hebrews 13:15 are only a few examples of his admonishing the church to give thanks to God in all occasions. South African pastor Andrew Murray wrote, "Let us thank God heartily as often as we pray that we have His Spirit in us to teach us to pray. Thanksgiving will draw our hearts out to God and keep us engaged with Him; it will take our attention from ourselves and give the Spirit room in our hearts."[123]

As a child of God, a son, a brother, a husband, a father, and a missionary pastor, there have been days when, in my

---

[121] C.H. Spurgeon, Spurgeon's Sermons Volume 18 (1872) found in sermon preached on Dec. 8, 1872.

[122] Richard Foster and James Bryan Smith, Devotional Classics, (Harper Collins, 2005), 87.

[123] Andrew Murray, *The Prayer Life*, (Simon & Schuster, 2013), 31.

attempts to pray, I only could muster a muttering of thanks. I can always hear the chorus of the old hymn written by Johnson Oatman: "Count your blessings, name them one by one. Count your blessings, see what God hath done." I must admit that on more than one occasion I have done just that. I take a piece of paper and start with the number one and make a list of what I am thankful for that God has done. As English Puritan preacher Thomas Watson reminds us, "How may we know that we are rightly thankful? When we are careful to register God's mercy... Physicians say the memory is the first thing that decays."[124]

My children have taught me volumes concerning the exponential life. The simplicity and innocence they bring to the conversations we have about God make me understand why they were one of Jesus' favorite sermon illustrations. This prayer of thanksgiving has been a fixture in my family's mealtime prayers for as long as I can remember. My father would always slide in a "thank you Lord for our many blessings." For a season we found ourselves eating with my parents quite often and all of us were accustomed to those simple and sincere prayers. My daughter heard something the rest of us didn't. She curiously asked, which ones are our "mini" blessings. And this innocent question changed my view of thankfulness.

---

[124] Thomas Watson, *The Godly Man's Picture,* (Reformed Church Publications, 2015), 101.

For that childlike reason I choose to leave no leaf unturned in my thankfulness. I list the most minute details, even the ones that may cause me to laugh and chuckle at their absurdity and insignificance. At times these seemingly silly efforts at thanksgiving have served as an integral part of my prayer life. I have learned that there is just as much power in thanking God for our "mini" blessing, as we will find in our many blessings. In recounting blessings received, I strengthen my confidence and enable myself to wait trustingly for what I asked for in prayer.

God does not necessarily change my situation, but each time he changes *me*. In true biblical prayer, whether praying the Lord's Prayer, the Psalms, interceding for needs, casting our cares, or simple thanksgiving, we approach God with the attitude that English theologian John R.W. Stott demonstrated when he wrote, "In prayer we do not 'prevail on' God, but rather prevail on ourselves to submit to God."[125] In order for prayer to be genuine, we must focus not on what we want, but what God wants. During my journey in the exponential life I have learned to no longer pray to simply pray, but to pray because I want to know more intimately the goodness of God.

---

125 Anna Wierzbicka, *What did Jesus Mean?: Explaining the Sermon on the Mount and the Parables in Simple and Universal Human Concepts*, (Oxford University Press, 2001), 188.

Jesus' promise, Paul's power in prayer, and your personal Pentecost

I ALWAYS HAD this image of the Holy Spirit as something akin to a live wire to be grabbed at times so it would flow as a conductor when the juice was on and the conditions were right. In the apostle Paul's writing, I see something completely different. As Bernard of Clairvaux explained:

> The man who is wise, therefore, will see his life as more like a reservoir than a canal. The canal simultaneously pours out what it receives; the reservoir retains the water till it is filled, then discharges the overflow without loss to itself ... Today there are many in the Church who act like canals, the reservoirs are far too rare ... You too must learn to await this fullness before pouring out your gifts, do not try to be more generous than God.[126]

We live, we minister, we speak, we respond, we give, we forgive, we extend mercy, we pray, we deny ourselves, we worship, and we listen only insofar as we're able to draw from this deep well. One way this reservoir of our souls is filled is by praying in the Spirit.

---

[126] Bernard of Clairvaux, *On the Song of Songs*, (Cistercian Publications, 1971), Sermon 18.

Now those of us who are native to the Charismatic stream of Christendom do not struggle to believe that the Holy Spirit is active in our daily lives and working in us and through us. We must take a moment to consider the place of the third person of the trinity in our journey to the exponential life. Let us first clear the air. I must admit that when we talk about being Pentecostal or being filled with the Spirit, most people pause because of someone or something weird they have experienced along the way. I want to establish clearly that the Holy Spirit is not weird, obnoxious, out of control, or embarrassing, and he doesn't make anyone else that way.

The Word of God tells us that the Holy Spirit is a gentleman awaiting our invitation (Luke 11:13). He can be resisted (Acts 7:5). He can be grieved (Ephesians 4:30). Yet He is in control at all times and never disorderly (1 Corinthians 14:40, 43). And always empowering (Acts 1:8). Even so, he is not in the weird business. For those of you who are part of the Charismatic stream of Christianity, I make a heartfelt appeal. Specifically for those who feel the need to demand that the work of the Holy Spirit must be outlandish or weird: Please stop it!

Praying in the Spirit is the fulfillment of a promise found throughout the Old Testament centuries before Jesus arrived on earth. Peter pointed to this again in Acts 2 when he explained that the phenomenon witnessed on the Day of Pentecost was nothing more than "what was spoken by the prophet Joel: 'In the last days, God says, I will pour out my Spirit on all people.'"[127] The disciples knew from the Old Testament prophecy that this promise was inclusive to "sons and daughters" and to young as well as old[128] and given regardless of race, gender, or social status. Far before these became talking points for campaign trails, the Holy Spirit in one fell swoop leveled the playing field in the Church. The Church must understand that the operation of the power of God, the prophecies, the visions, the dreams, healings, works of faith, and what Paul would call the "gifts of the spirit" are not limited to any one class, race, or gender, but are available to all.

The Holy Spirit is inclusive and empowering. He teaches, guides, and fills us with spiritual fervor for the lost. Almost everyone wants such an experience. Yet there is a part of Pentecost that can act as a stumbling block: speaking in tongues. This evidence of Pentecost was the common experience throughout the Book of Acts that followed the filling of the Holy Spirit. All the personal Pentecosts that would take place — in the Upper Room, in the house of Cornelius, and among the Ephesian believers, the one experienced by the apostle Paul and the Corinthian church — they occurred regardless of race, gender, or social status.

They were all empowered, taught, and guided. Ultimately they were all filled with passion for the lost. You

---

[127] Acts 2:17-21, NIV

[128] Ibid

may say "yes" to the proposition, but amend it with "yeah, but..." Some may say they would love the Holy Spirit, but do not want to speak in tongues. Some Christians I have met treat speaking in tongues as if it is a bad side effect, like male pattern baldness, fever, or nausea that causes them to completely abandon their willingness and waiting on the Holy Spirit.

Those who do so are missing out without ever giving God a full opportunity to work in their lives. Let's try looking at this not as a side effect, but as an amazing opportunity we have been given to engage or connect with God. Tongues is simply praying in a language you do not know. Isn't that something that crazy people do? Those who are emotionally unhinged? Not according to a *New York Times* piece from 2006: "Contrary to what may be a common perception, studies suggest that people who speak in tongues rarely suffer from mental problems...those who engaged in the practice were more emotionally stable than those who did not."[129]

Many ask whether speaking in tongues is unbiblical. It is really anything but. Those who deny the active work of the Holy Spirit in our daily lives through speaking in tongues are also usually the same ones who say that God no longer actively works miracles. To reach their conclusion, God somehow gave up his ability to do the charismatic work

---

[129] The *New York Times* article titled "A Neuroscientific Look at Speaking in Tongues," Nov. 7, 2006.

through the Holy Spirit. It takes theological backflips to come to the conclusion that God no longer works in certain ways. New Testament scholar N. T. Wright states, "Some parts of the Church take a 'cessationist' view that the gift of tongues ended with the closure of Scripture. Again, that goes back to 1 Corinthians 13, where Paul says where there have been tongues, 'they shall cease,'[130] but he doesn't actually say when."[131] Even the great Reformed theologian J. I. Packer admits that speaking in tongues does in fact have "its place in the inescapable pluriformity of Christian experience, in which the varied makeup of both cultures and individuals is reflected by a wide range of devotional styles." And "none should forbid them their practice."[132] Look to Church father John Cassian who advised us not to take Paul's literal words for granted. He said, "This last suggestion seems quite absurd to me. For it ought not to be believed that the Holy Spirit would have said something through the apostle in passing and for no reason. And therefore let us treat them again individually..."[133] See exactly what he said.

---

[130] KJV

[131] Wright, Thom (2021, March 29) *Does the gift of tongues still operate today? N.T. Wright gives his answer.* Premier Christianity https://www.premierchristianity.com/home/does-the-gift-of-tongues-still-operate-today-nt-wright-gives-his-answer/2194.article.

[132] J.I. Packer, *Keep in Step with the Spirit: Finding Fullness in Our Walk with God*, (Baker Books, 2005), 183.

[133] John Cassian, *The Conferences*, (The Newman Press, 1997), 337.

When we start peeling back Paul's exponential life, it is quickly evident that the apostle was in fact a full contact Charismatic-Pentecostal. He confessed in 1 Corinthians 14:18, "I thank God that I speak in tongues more than all of you." So it is clear that this man of unrivaled influence in the production of our modern theology spoke in tongues and was not ashamed to do so. And he was an advocate of the experience in the lives of every Christian when he confessed, "I would like every one of you to speak in tongues" in that same chapter of 1 Corinthians. He was so dedicated to the role of tongues in the Christian life that he gave a forceful exhortation that we "not forbid speaking in tongues."[134]

Let me give several biblical reasons why you should want to speak in tongues. It helps us to pray. In Romans 8:28, we find the preface to the famous promise that says, "And we know that all things work together for our good." But look at what Paul taught just before that in verses 26-27:

> Likewise the Spirit helps us in our weakness. For we do not know what to pray for as we ought, but the Spirit himself intercedes for us with groanings too deep for words. And he who searches hearts knows what is the

[134] 1 Corinthians 14:39

> mind of the Spirit, because the Spirit intercedes for the saints according to the will of God.[135]

In a recent interview, N. T. Wright testified, "Many, many times, when I have needed to pray into a particular situation, but had no idea of what I should be praying for, the use of tongues in private prayer has enabled me to hold people in situations within the love of God."[136]

Speaking in tongues gives us a direct line to God. In 1 Corinthians 14:2,[137] Paul clearly states, "For anyone who speaks in a tongue does not speak to people but to God. Indeed, no one understands them; they utter mysteries by the Spirit." The practice also builds us up, encourages us, and brings the peace that Jesus promised would follow the arrival of the Holy Spirit. As Paul said in 1 Corinthians 14:4a,[138] "Anyone who speaks in a tongue edifies themselves." In a recent BBC article, the Archbishop of Canterbury, Justin Welby, who is the leader of the worldwide Anglican Church, unashamedly admitted that he prays in tongues every morning during his prayer time. He said: "In my own prayer life, and as part of my daily disci-

---

[135] ESV

[136] Wright, N. T. (2021, March 29). *Does the gift of tongues still operate today? N.T. Wright gives his answer*. Premier Christianity. https://www.premierchristianity.com/home/does-the-gift-of-tongues-still-operate-today-nt-wright-gives-his-answer/2194.article.

[137] NIV

[138] Ibid

pline, I pray in tongues every day — not as an occasional thing but as part of daily prayer."[139] If our ultimate goal of prayer is to develop an ongoing conversation with God, this can be seen as a unique opportunity given by God to intimately commune with him.

It is clear that Paul held two separate purposes for tongues. One was for corporate worship in which the message needed to be translated and the other for private prayer that served for personal edification. I in no way think that the goal is to live in a trance-like ecstatic state of incoherence. I believe tongues have a place in our journey to an exponential life, filling a unique role in our growth, much like a supernatural artesian well that will continue to fill the reservoir of our soul or in Paul's words, in a state of being constantly filled.[140] But British theologian Donald Gee gave a wise warning when he wrote, "Tongues are a perfectly lawful outlet for deep emotion in the spirit, but they are not to be a substitute for more intelligible forms of prayer and praise."[141]

That is the reason I have listed several more traditional forms of daily prayer. Tongues should never be viewed as

---

[139] Welby, J. (2019, Jan 21). I pray in tongues every day, says the archbishop of Canterbury. *The Guardian.* https://www.theguardian.com/uk-news/2019/jan/21/i-pray-in-tongues-every-day-says-archbishop-of-canterbury.

[140] Ephesians 5:18

[141] Donald Gee, *All With One Accord*, (Gospel Publishing House, 1961), 39.

an end; like all the other on-ramps, it is solely a means, a means to a deeper experience, and an empowered life. Ultimately it helps to lead us to true exponential life. Yet due to personal preference, many continue to ask, why should I want to speak in tongues? It is more important to ask, if you had the opportunity to pray in tongues each day, why wouldn't you do so?

The destination of prayer, in any of its forms, is very clear and unbelievably practical. "We should have no doubt that our prayer is acceptable and heard, and we must leave to God the measure, manner, time, and place, for God will surely do what is right."[142] The man or woman who takes this on-ramp will inevitably be led into a deep sense of humility that is birthed when our childlike faith intersects with our simple trust. It takes humility to ask for your needs and for the needs of others. It takes humility to confess your weaknesses. It takes humility to forgive and to be forgiven. It takes humility to recognize your dependence on the strength of another. It takes humility to wait. It takes humility to pray.

Prayer takes our focus off of us and places it onto God. Pastor and author Rick Warren said, "Humility is not thinking less of yourself, it is thinking of yourself less."[143]

---

142 Martin Luther, *A Treatise on Good Works,* (Classical Ethereal Library), 37.

143 Rick Warren, *The Purpose Driven Life: What on Earth am I here for?* (Zondervan, 2002), 38

That is exactly what prayer is about. This humility leads us to meekness and to a state of bridled strength. The bridle on a horse allows a 90-pound jockey to direct a 1,300-pound gathering of a horse's muscle and strength. We, too, through prayer, give up our rights voluntarily to our Heavenly Father. Andrew Murray said :

> Humility is the only soil in which the graces root; the lack of humility is the sufficient explanation of every defect and failure Humility is not so much a grace or virtue along with others; it is the root of all, because it alone takes the right attitude before God, and allows Him as God to do all.[144]

This humility does not place us in a posture of weakness, but instead in a true posture of exponential power. "No one can believe how powerful prayer is and what it can affect, except those who have learned it by experience."[145]

---

[144] Andrew Murray, *Humility: The Journey Towards Holiness*, (Bethany House Publishers, 2001), 17.

[145] Martin Luther, *Table Talk Essay, Antiquariaus* (2021). CCCXXVIII.

Make it personal

1. When and where do you usually pray?

2. Do you feel comfortable honestly expressing yourself in prayer? If not, what is holding you back?

3. What forms does your prayer take? Aloud? Written word? In thought? Corporately with a liturgy?

4. Make a list of the typical content of your prayer. What takes up most of your prayer life?

Paradoxical Imperatives for Relating to Others

6. On-Ramp of Wilderness

I REMEMBER on a few occasions staying home from school because I was sick. In those days, before cable, our television could only pick up three stations, and those only with the help of a generous amount of tinfoil on the rabbit-ear antenna. Unlike our endless entertainment opportunities today, I only had the option of watching soap operas or game shows. As a young boy I always went with the latter. At 10 years old, I guessed the price of a washer and dryer set. I told the dealer to "hit me" with another card in my attempt to reach 21 without busting. I mumbled "big money, no whammies" as I put myself in the chair of the contestant. One of my favorites was the game show *Pyramid,* where the contestant could walk away with $10,000. In those days, that was enough to buy a house. A key aspect of the game was to give hints to lead a teammate to guess a particular word.

Now imagine that we are teammates and I give you the clues, "solitude," "silence," and "stillness." What would you guess? Prison? Punishment? Confinement? Hell? What if I said, "A place you are created to run toward, but constantly run from." Regrettably, too many of us never realize the beauty and the transforming power of the answer. The word is *wilderness.* We need only to look at pop culture to see this word is continually painted with unappealing colors. We are afraid that if we are ever required to spend a day in the wilderness, we will find ourselves befriending a sports ball and talking incoherently to ourselves *a la* Tom Hanks in *Cast Away*.

In John 15, Jesus teaches that a servant is not greater than his master and that, as his disciples, we are destined to share in his experiences, good and bad. We can expect that in following the on-ramps Jesus modeled, we will eventually find ourselves in the wilderness just as he did. The wilderness I am speaking of has little to do with the number of trees surrounding us. It can be found even in the middle of an urban setting, but will always be characterized by solitude, silence, and stillness. We see this in the example of Jesus' life:

> He withdrew from there in a boat to a desolate place by himself. After he had dismissed the crowds, he went up on the mountain by himself to pray. And after sending away the crowds, he got into the boat and went to the region of Magadan.[146]

What was it that he constantly sought? Crowds? Larger venues? The limelight? A better platform to be completely understood? Not at all! It was solitude, silence, and stillness.

[146] Matthew 14:13, 23 and 15:39, ESV

He sought out the wilderness. We can clearly see the well-worn path that he left as an example beginning in Matthew 4 where Jesus was "driven" to the wilderness by the Holy Spirit to pray and overcome temptation. It is obvious that "it was his will to live his life in an ordinary rhythm of interaction and solitude."[147] And because it was so central to his life, he introduced his disciples to this place in Luke 5 and he sought it out no matter how good things were going, even following some of his greatest miracles. It seemed as the crowds grew, he could hear the wilderness crying out to him even more.

Solitude is the state of being alone and in a higher state of silence. It is a place we go to do our deepest work:

> For what purpose does he go up into the mountain? To teach us that loneliness and retirement is good, when we are to pray to God. With this view, you see he is continually withdrawing into the wilderness, and there often spends the whole night in prayer, teaching us earnestly to seek such quietness in our prayers, as the time and place may offer. For the wilderness is the mother of quiet: it is a calm and a harbor, delivering us from all turmoils.[148]

---

[147] Manlio Simonetti, *Ancient Christian Commentary on Scripture: Matthew 1-13*, (InterVarsity Press, 2014), 6.

[148] Philip Schaff, *Nicene and Post-Nicene Fathers: First Series, Volume X St. Chrysostom*, (Cosimo Inc, 2007, 310.

It was a place he discovered after being driven there by the Holy Spirit. It was a place he took his disciples so that they, too, could learn its importance. It is the place he is calling us to go if we want to live the exponential life. As Eugene Peterson knew, "When we want to let the life of Christ make a revolutionary impact on our life, we go to the desert."[149]

What happens in the wilderness?

IN THE SOLITUDE, silence, and the stillness of the wilderness, we are reminded of our true goal, which lies in contrast to what our noisy world would have us believe. It is not to shout louder, hoping that God will listen to our prayer. It is stepping away from our busyness into silence, all while leaning in closer to hear God's voice found in the stillness:

> Especially in the Hebrew Bible, wilderness is the privileged site where God comforts the Hebrew people or their representatives at times of crisis in their lives. In the wilderness God calls and leads them to decisions and

---

[149] Eugene Peterson, *A Month of Sundays: Thirty-One Days of Wrestling with Matthew, Mark, Luke, and John,* (Crown Publishing, 2019), 47.

> witnesses their shortcomings; and God disciplines and punishes them for their sin and rebellion. Throughout the gospels wilderness is important for Jesus as a place of encounter with the Father.[150]

We continually see Jesus following the same path to solitude as the prophets and spiritual leaders before him.

We can observe the position of solitude on full display in 1 Kings 19:11-12 with the prophet Elijah:

> Then He said, "Go out, and stand on the mountain before the Lord." And behold, the Lord passed by, and a great and strong wind tore into the mountains and broke the rocks in pieces before the Lord, but the Lord was not in the wind; and after the wind an earthquake, but the Lord was not in the earthquake; and after the earthquake a fire, but the Lord was not in the fire; and after the fire a still small voice.

This was apparent in the life of the greatest prophet, John the Baptist. The wilderness is the place for prayer and divine listening for the "still small voice." Missionary Frank Laubach reminds us that in the wilderness we remember that, "listening to God is far more important than giving

---

150 Marlena Graves, *A Beautiful Disaster: Finding Hope in the Midst of Brokenness*, (Brazos Publishing, 2014), 9.

Him your ideas."[151] Some may think that it is limited to mountain retreats or desert monasteries, but this is wholly untrue, because solitude is a posture as much as it is a place. It is a reality that certain places can indeed draw us in, but if we are intent on seeking it out, it can be found in a subway or a sidewalk, just as well as in a cathedral on the side of a mountain.

In the wilderness we will all be tested. If we allow it, it can reveal the depths of our commitment as well as the insincerity of our shallowness. As Church father John Chrysostom knew,

> You see how the Spirit led him, not into a city or public arena, but into a wilderness. In this desolate place, the Spirit extended the devil an occasion to test him, not only by hunger, but also by loneliness, for it is there most especially that the devil assails us, when he sees us left alone and by ourselves. In this same way did he also confront Eve in the beginning, having caught her alone and apart from her husband.[152]

We are who we truly are in the silence of solitude, not in the noise of busyness.

---

[151] Liz Thompson, *God Whispers*, (First Edition Publishers, 2013), 38.
[152] Thomas C. Oden, Christopher A. Hall, *Ancient Christian Commentary on Scripture: Mark*, (InterVarsity Press, 2014), 16.

In the wilderness, we find separation from negative influences. There it is easier to see just how influential the "mob" has become to our outlook on life. Many Christians and potential disciples have found themselves swept up in the modern current of understanding and now behave as though they are "of the world." This is a common occurrence for those who live day in and day out inside of a community. We have a tendency to become products of our environment. According to research by social psychologist David McClelland of Harvard, the people you habitually associate with determine as much as 95% of your success or failure in life.[153]

Some fall prey to their mob of choice and find themselves living as they never intended. It becomes clear just how much leverage "they" have been given in our lives, channeling our thoughts, twisting our responses, and manipulating our actions, whoever "they" may be. Groups of individuals are collectively induced to do things they would otherwise never do. When we find ourselves in the midst of a mob, we tend to feel invisible and, as a result, we are susceptible to compromise our values and principles.

Seeking out the wilderness is the foremost way to divorce ourselves from the abusive relationship we have with hurry. Dallas Willard teaches that "hurry is the great enemy of spiritual life in our day. You must ruthlessly eliminate hurry

---

153 Darren Hardy, *The Compound Effect*, (Vanguard Press, 2012), 127.

from your life."[154] If we could record the soundtrack of our hurried and noisy lives, it would seem like a cacophony, with no rhythm or reason. This is a sad reality because our lives are intended to be marvelous works filled with music that proceeds from God's rhythm and his reason. Solitude serves as a pause in our process and stands in opposition to our chaotic noise-filled lives. Consequently, solitude — when consistently sought out and practiced in the same way as Jesus did — causes our lives to take a more intentional form analogous to Wolfgang Mozart's explanation of composition: "The music is not in the notes, but in the silence between."[155] In the wilderness, we will come to realize that in spite of what our world tells us, busyness does not equal value or importance. Actually in the wilderness we will encounter the truest form of rest.

The Spirit will lead you and, if needed, even drive you to the wilderness so that you can wrestle with your temptations and with the enemy of your soul. Eventually, you may even come to wrestle with yourself. Wilderness is a place many fear because in our aloneness we find that our only company is the person who has done us the most damage. It is hard to point fingers and judge when no one else is

---

[154] John Ortberg, *Soul Keeping: Caring For the Most Important Part of You*, (Zondervan, 2014), 157.

[155] DK, *Music: The Definitive Visual History*, (DK Publishing, UK, 2013), 138t.

around. There we come to grips with who we really are and the warped facets of our heart.

The wilderness, although a challenge at first, will become a place of healing for those who seek it out. As author Marlena Graves notes,

> The wilderness has a way of curing our illusions about ourselves and teaching us to depend more and more on God. When we first enter, we're convinced we've entered the bowels of hell. But on our pilgrimage, we discover that the desert drips with the divine. We discover that desert land is fertile ground for spiritual activity, transformation, and renewal.[156]

A drive through the southwest corner of the United States can seem like a sparse and arid landscape when only viewed at 70 mph from a car window. Yet if you just stop for a while, the beauty of the wilderness starts to peak through the elements. Only after our eyes have adjusted can we focus on the details that make up our surroundings. Then we see the shadowed tones, the brilliant multiplicity of hues reflected on that landscape, and the wondrously colorful blooms that fill each shaded crevice.

The 19th century Scottish preacher Andrew Bonar spoke similarly on the topic:

---

[156] Marlena Graves, *A Beautiful Disaster*, (Baker Publishing, 2014), 7.

> In order to grow in grace, men must be much alone. It is not in society that the soul grows most vigorously. It is in the desert that the dew falls freshest and the air is purest. The back side of the desert is where men and things, the world and self, present circumstances and their influences, are all valued at what they are really worth. There it is, and there alone, that you will find a divinely adjusted balance in which to weigh all around you and within you.[157]

Jesus spent his life dismissing the crowds so he could do real ministry. Yet here we are 2,000 years later making every attempt to draw crowds because in large part we have forgotten how real ministry happens. The danger of crowds is the delusion of success they can produce in church leaders and pastors. If we are to ever inherit the exponential life that Jesus promised, we will need to embrace the wilderness as Jesus did.

How do we find our wilderness?

LIKE JESUS, if we are to enter into the wilderness, the wilderness must be sought out. Set a time or maybe even a

---

[157] L. B. Cowman, *Streams in the Desert,* (Zondervan, 1996), 606.

few times a day with the sole purpose of stealing away for a few moments of silence. This will create a space for some of the other on-ramps so they can be integrated as well. You may have to do it on your break time or lunch hour. Initially, you may feel like you are wasting time, but God seems to be closer to those who are willing to "waste time" for him. This is because wilderness creates a "thin place" in our soul. I structure my time in coordination with the prayer rhythm honored by Jesus and his disciples as faithful Jews (Psalm 55:17, Daniel 6:10). The custom was developed during exile and brought back when the Israelites returned to rebuild the temple. It included at least three sacred pauses each day. While not chiseled in stone, it is a good starting place.

For me, these times are in the early morning, around lunch, and before bed. These small moments of five to 10 minutes keep me on course. Determine the time you will enter into the wilderness and the place you will retreat in your effort to be alone with God. I have used prayer chapels, churches of all denominations, the inside of my car, a concrete sidewalk in a city park, a bench under a shade tree, or the corner booth of a coffee shop or restaurant. Jesus even designates the sacred space found inside a closet as sufficient to be classified as a Wilderness in Matthew 6:6. You could say these are mini wilderness experiences.

Once you have integrated the concept of seeking out wilderness in your daily life, you likely will find that you are drawn to it. It will call out to you. It will become a highlight in your daily grind. Eventually, as this on-ramp stretches you, you will find out what naturalist Edward Abbey did when he observed, "Wilderness is not a luxury, but a necessity of the human spirit."[158]

You will press to take more and more time in the wilderness. I have reached a place where I strive to block off my time in solitude, silence, and stillness. This inner pull toward the wilderness and what it offers actually allows for a much easier merge onto two of the other on-ramps found in the exponential life: sabbath and beholding. It also becomes the place of greatest listening and prayer, thus uniting four of our on-ramps in a common theme.

If we are to develop our wilderness experience we must refuse to be "wait" watchers. Most of us are so wrapped up in a schedule that opportunities for solitude, silence, and stillness are brushed aside. I have found that in wandering into the wilderness I must be willing to wait. That takes planning, and for those on time restraints, it means scheduling an appointment to make wilderness happen. Waiting is the hardest part of the spiritual life and the process of spiritual formation. It is certainly true when we are talking about the wilderness.

The most important aspect in finding wilderness is simply the realization that in one way or another, God wants to

---

[158] Edward Abbey, *Desert Solitaire*, (Ballantine Books, 1985), 169.

get you all alone, so that he can talk with you and give you rest. In the wilderness God spoke to Moses through a burning bush, an encounter that changed his life and all of history. In the wilderness, God proved his faithfulness to Israel. In the wilderness, God passed by the cave, and the prophet Elijah heard the "still small voice" of the Lord. In the wilderness, King David found refuge from his enemies. In the wilderness, Jesus overcame his greatest temptations. And in the wilderness, we will find the direction, faithfulness, encouragement, protection, and power we need to journey toward exponential life. As Brennan Manning found, we must find a wilderness "of some kind (your backyard will do)" so that we may "come into a personal experience of the awesome love of God."[159]

The dark night of our spiritual wilderness

THERE IS A SECOND kind of wilderness that seems to find us rather than needing to be sought out. It is the "spiritual valley" or "a dry season." It is a place where we feel alone spiritually, as if God has left us or turned away. It is a place of physical or emotional pain. This wilderness is usually filled with a constant companion, the swirling unan-

[159] Brennan Manning, *The Ragamuffin Gospel: Good News for the Bedraggled, Beat-Up, and Burnt Out*, (Multnomah, 1990), 36.

swered question *why*. Why did this happen to me? Why is God not doing things the way I expected him to? Why was the other person promoted and not me? Why was I rejected? And on and on it hovers, still unanswered. We even see Jesus' unanswered why echoed in the prophetic 22nd Psalm. David wrote:

> My God, my God, why have you forsaken me? Why are you so far from saving me, from the words of my groaning? O my God, I cry by day, but you do not answer, and by night, but I find no rest.[160]

Jesus pointed to these unavoidable wildernesses when he concluded the Sermon on the Mount in Matthew 7:

> Therefore whoever hears these sayings of Mine, and does them, I will liken him to a wise man who built his house on the rock: and the rain descended, the floods came, and the winds blew and beat on that house; and it did not fall, for it was founded on the rock.
>
> But everyone who hears these sayings of Mine, and does not do them, will be like a foolish man who built his house on the sand: and the rain descended, the floods

160 Psalm 22:1-2, ESV

> came, and the winds blew and beat on that house; and it fell. And great was its fall.[161]

The rains are inevitable and certain in this life. Loss, pain, separation, unmet expectations, and death are all part of our human story. No one has ever been able to avoid them. Even with this established fact, many have been shipwrecked in their faith because they thought no one before had suffered as they were suffering. Eventually they arrived at a place of unmitigated anger toward God as a result of something unavoidable and inevitable that they felt was unfair.

We come by this reaction honestly, as part of our neurological makeup, surging from one of the areas geared toward survival and self-preservation. We are designed to seek out happiness and comfort. Augustine stated, "We are certainly in a common class with the beasts; every action of animal life is concerned with seeking bodily pleasure and avoiding pain."[162] Somehow, this subtle drive to preserve ourselves gives way to a self-serving nature that will do anything to avoid whatever does not offer immediate happiness and guaranteed comfort.

As I previously mentioned, this is a dangerous state of mind for a disciple. Troubles happen in our lives. Sands

---

[161] Matthew 7:24-27

[162] Augustine, *The Problem of Free Choice*, Ancient Christian Writers, (The Newman Press, 1955), 53.

shift, winds blow, things crash down, and, if our outlook isn't realistic, we feel somehow God is not fair because he doesn't offer us endless supplies of happiness and comfort we so passionately desire.

Author Philip Yancey learned this when he met a man named Douglas, whom he interviewed for his book *Disappointment with God.* Yancey shared the story of Douglas, a devout Christian whose wife was diagnosed with breast cancer. Later, Douglas suffered myriad physical challenges due to a traffic accident with a drunk driver. Yet rather than shaking his fist in God's face as a result of the unavoidable wilderness, he confessed that as a result of reading the Book of Job he had learned to:

> feel free to curse the unfairness of life and to vent all my grief and anger. But I believe God feels the same way about that accident — grieved and angry. I don't blame him for what happened. I have learned to see beyond the physical reality of this world to the spiritual reality. We tend to think, "Life should be fair because God is fair." But God is not life. And if I confuse God with the physical reality of life — by expecting constant good health, for example — then I set myself up for a crashing disappointment. God's existence, even his love for me, does not depend on my good health. Frankly, I've had more time and opportunity to work on my relationship

> with God during my impairment than before.[163]

Douglas then challenged Yancey "go home and read again the story of Jesus. Was life fair to him? For me, the cross demolished for all time the basic assumption that life will be fair."[164]

When we realize that sorrow and pain are part of the experience of simply being alive, we understand life isn't fair. These troubling times that are unavoidable will be seen as they are in eternity, the "thin places" referenced earlier by our Celtic forefathers. In this arid land God is close and ever present. When we realize that hardship places us in an undeniable position, these times become less troublesome as we experience greater intimacy with God: when life doesn't go as we planned; when our short-term desires for happiness and comfort are left unmet by the greater plan of our Creator; when in an act of obedience we find ourselves leaving something or someplace that has provided us with our desired levels of both happiness and comfort, only to find ourselves temporarily wandering in the not-yet desert without a place to land. Yet notice the number of times in the gospels that Jesus himself was drawn to the tears caused by the unfairness of life. Mary Magdalene (Luke 7:36-50); the widow of Nain (Luke 7:11-17); Jarius for his daughter (Luke 8:40-56); Lazarus's sisters (John 11:1-37).

---

[163] Philip Yancey, *Disappointment with God,* (Zondervan, 2015) 194.
[164] Ibid. 195.

John of the Cross taught us that this thin place caused by the unfairness of life didn't need to be to be feared or avoided because it is a place of deeper intimacy with God. Psalm 34:18 promises, "The Lord is close to the broken-hearted and saves those who are crushed in spirit."[165] Eugene Peterson translated it: "If your heart is broken, you'll find God right there; if you're kicked in the gut, he'll help you catch your breath."[166] In reality, John of the Cross learned to enjoy the nearness of God and the certainty of his presence in the night. "Love consists not in feeling great things but in having great detachment and in suffering for the Beloved."[167] This reality of a true love relationship based on sacrifice formed the foundation for the 16th century Spanish poet's most famous revelation, "The Dark Night of the Soul." This realization is a hallmark evident in the lives of the disciples, as well as anyone who commits to living the exponential life.

It would be easier if somehow we could learn from the suffering of others, but alas it is unlikely to happen. Only through our own personal suffering can we learn:

> God uses the desert of the soul — our suffering and difficulties, our pain, our dark nights (call them what you

[165] NIV

[166] Psalm 34:18, MSG

[167] John of the Cross, *The Collected Works of Saint John of the Cross (ICS Publications, 1991)*, 93 .

> will) — to form us, to make us beautiful souls. He redeems what we might deem our living hells, if we allow him. The hard truth, then, is this: everyone who follows Jesus is eventually called into the desert.[168]

In this dark place we learn to examine ourselves to see if we have strayed from obedience in the path God has laid before us.

This is where we listen intently to his voice as a result of the pain we are feeling. C. S. Lewis wrote, "Pain insists upon being attended to. God whispers to us in our pleasures, speaks in our consciences, but shouts in our pains. It is his megaphone to rouse a deaf world."[169] It is the place where we learn about true faith — which walks by faith and not by sight — and where we learn to trust in the goodness of God. Here we experience firsthand that "faith is a living, daring confidence in God's grace, so sure and certain that a man could stake his life on it a thousand times."[170]

Most of us struggle to deal with pain. Some struggle to grasp why we have pain if God is love. Those of us who have experienced and learned to embrace the wilderness of the dark night can attest that these things happen so that he can reveal his love for us and draw us closer to himself. It is

---

168 Marlena Graves, A Beautiful Disaster, (Baker Publishing, 2014) 16.

169 C. S. Lewis, *The Problem of Pain,* USA, Collins, 2012, 93.

170 Steven Lawson, *Holman Old Testament Commentary - Psalms*, USA, (B&H Publishing, 2004), 29.

not that we become spiritual sadomasochists who seek pain just for the heck of it, but we do learn that pain is a part of God's exponential process.

As Charles Spurgeon confessed, "I am certain that I never did grow in grace one-half so much anywhere as I have upon the bed of pain."[171] The realization that our negative situations can have a positive outcome in our lives can shape our response to pain. "We all know people who have been made much meaner and more irritable and more intolerable to live with by suffering: it is not right to say that all suffering perfects. It only perfects one type of person — the one who accepts the call of God in Christ Jesus."[172]

This common wilderness will lead us to proclaim with the apostle Paul in Romans 5:3-5:

> We also glory in tribulations, knowing that tribulation produces perseverance; and perseverance, character; and character, hope. Now hope does not disappoint, because the love of God has been poured out in our hearts by the Holy Spirit who was given to us.

As a result of our growth in these times in the emotional wilderness, we learn that "in tribulation" we need to "im-

---

[171] Mary Ann Jefferys, Sayings of Spurgeon, (*Christian History* magazine #29, 1991).

[172] Sarah Kay, *Pieces of Glass: A Moment of Tragedy, A Lifetime of Faith*, (Zondervan, 2009), 94.

mediately draw near to God with confidence" because we can be assured that we "will receive strength, enlightenment, and instruction."[173] When we find God in the dark, in our interior solitude, our inner silence, or in the stillness of our pain, it is no longer a scary place.

There are two main categories of wilderness: the voluntary, which is more literal and physical, versus the unavoidable, which is internal and emotional. I have found the former is a product of choice that seems to prepare me for the latter, which often stem from uncontrollable circumstances. The solitude, silence, and stillness we integrate into our lives create a ballast for the seasons when we sail into the storm of the Dark Night. Our times in the wilderness — whether a voluntary or unavoidable — will at first glance seem sparse and arid, maybe even dead and despondent. Yet we must understand that just beneath the surface there is endemic beauty that can only be found in these harsh landscapes. Only when we choose to stay a while, to embrace the wilderness, will our eyes adjust to our surroundings and its God-given beauty will start to creep through. This internal adjustment of our outlook will eventually lead us to a place of peace.

Paul helps us to see this real place of peace in Philippians chapter 4,

[173] John of the Cross, *The Collected Works of Saint John of the Cross*, (ICS Publications,1991), 90.

> ...the peace of God, which surpasses all understanding, will guard your hearts and minds through Christ Jesus.
>
> Finally, brethren, whatever things are true, whatever things are noble, whatever things are just, whatever things are pure, whatever things are lovely, whatever things are of good report, if there is any virtue and if there is anything praiseworthy — meditate on these things. The things which you learned and received and heard and saw in me, these do, and the God of peace will be with you.[174]

This peace is found in the silence, solitude, and stillness of the wilderness. It's not in the noise of society, the crowds, perfected performances, or in our constant state of hurry. This wilderness provides the space to do the work we need to do to fully submit ourselves to God. In doing so, we start a chain reaction of peace. When we are at peace with God, we will be at peace with ourselves. When we are at peace with ourselves, we can be at peace with others.[175]

---

[174] Philippians 4:7-9

[175] Thomas Merton, *The Living Bread*, (Farrar, Straus and Giroux, 2010), 14.

Make it personal

1. Is it difficult for you to be alone? Or do you feel like it is second nature?

2. How much of your average daily activity would you consider "wasted time?"

3. Which element of wilderness is more daunting for you? Silence? Stillness? Solitude?

4. Do you find it easy to avoid painful subjects rather than addressing them?

7. On-Ramp of Community

"I LOVE JESUS, I just don't like the Church" has become a common remark for those who have cooled on committing to a faith community. Now, as a result of the reality of the COVID-19 pandemic, some say, "I go. I just go online." That expression should sound as rare as a person pronouncing "I'm married, but we only talk online." Yet somehow it's not.

Although Jesus never said, "If you will be my disciple, go to church," he did make a lifelong habit of being in a faith community and of forming his small flock into more than simply a glorified dinner club. Realistically, we hear a mute discourse concerning this subject, but an examination of Jesus' actions as recorded in the Gospels reveals gathering with the faithful to be another of our imperatives.

In Luke 4, just as Jesus completed his 40 days in the wilderness, he returned to the Galilee of his youth. The record clearly seals the important place our faith community holds:

> Then Jesus returned in the power of the Spirit to Galilee, and news of Him went out through all the surrounding region. And He taught in their synagogues, being glorified by all.

> So He came to Nazareth, where He had been brought up. And as His custom was, He went into the synagogue on the Sabbath day, and stood up to read. And He was handed the book of the prophet Isaiah. And when He had opened the book, He found the place where it was written:
>
> > "The Spirit of the Lord is upon Me,
> > Because He has anointed Me
> > To preach the gospel to the poor;
> > He has sent Me to heal the brokenhearted,
> > To proclaim liberty to the captives
> > And recovery of sight to the blind,
> > To set at liberty those who are oppressed;
> > To proclaim the acceptable year of the Lord."
>
> Then He closed the book, and gave it back to the attendant and sat down. And the eyes of all who were in the synagogue were fixed on Him. And He began to say to them, "Today this Scripture is fulfilled in your hearing."[176]

This scene presents a number of revelations, both theological and practical.

[176] Luke 4:14-21

First, we note that as a result of his time in the wilderness through prayer, listening, and self-denial, he returned in the power of the Holy Spirit. He was no longer simply Mary and Joseph's boy or the carpenter's apprentice, but the Messiah sent by God, ready to be revealed. Next, he proclaimed his foretold place in history by introducing himself as the fulfillment of Isaiah's prophecy. But what does this moment reveal about how we should approach our faith communities?

Only when we start looking at the margins of this story do the words of Luke paint an additional picture for our application. He notes that he goes straightway from the wilderness to teach in the synagogues. Here Jesus started his ministry of preaching and proclaiming that the kingdom of God is at hand. We find him returning to minister in synagogues at least 10 times throughout the Gospels. A closer look shows it was more than simply the opening stage of Jesus' ever-expanding platform.

Verse 16 is usually overlooked in our eagerness to get to the "good stuff" of Jesus' proclamation: "So He came to Nazareth, where He had been brought up. And *as His custom was,*[177] He went into the synagogue on the Sabbath day, and stood up to read." Wait a minute. Did that say that Jesus made a habitual commitment to his faith community? The King of King and Lord of Lords, the Great "I AM,"

[177] Emphasis added.

the Lamb of God, the second member of the Holy Trinity, the Savior of the world, God with us, went to his faith community so often that Luke could confidently describe it as his custom. But weren't there gossips who attended the synagogue of Nazareth? Most likely. Especially when you consider that his mother was a virgin who got pregnant before marrying. Were there no hypocrites who belonged to Jesus' faith community? You bet there were. Why else would Nathanael feel compelled to reveal the lowered expectations when asked in John 1:46, "Can anything good come out of Nazareth?"

Did they accept the ministry of Jesus and give him more opportunities? Not in the way you may think. Just look at Matthew 13:

> When He had come to His own country, He taught them in their synagogue, so that they were astonished and said, "Where did this Man get this wisdom and these mighty works? Is this not the carpenter's son? Is not His mother called Mary? And His brothers James, Joses, Simon, and Judas? And His sisters, are they not all with us? Where then did this Man get all these things?" So they were offended at Him. But Jesus said to them, "A prophet is not without honor except in his own country and in his own house."[178]

[178] Matthew 13:53-58

For all the reasons we commonly give for drifting out of our faith community — backbiting gossip, hypocrisy, lack of recognition — Jesus didn't allow anything to phase his commitment to his community of faith.

Consider what exactly a synagogue looked like in Jesus' day. They formed to provide a place of daily prayer — specifically communal prayer — for the Jews spread far and wide around the Mediterranean Sea due to the breakup of Israel and Judah. The synagogue was a literal community of like-minded believers who gathered to study the Word of God so as to grow, pray corporately, and to represent God's hope for the unconverted world. These communities served as a place for the Jews, always considered foreigners anywhere they lived outside of Palestine, to be "in the world, but not of the world." They were different. God intended for them to be "set apart."

The Early Church was born and modeled after the synagogue, but changes have been made. The Word of God was eventually expanded. As the New Testament was written, focus shifted from Mosaic law to living a life of faith. But at the end of the day, its core remains the same for us as in Jesus' day. His synagogues *were* and our churches *are* to be a community gathered corporately to study the Word of God for spiritual growth, to pray, and to be a physical representation of God's presence on the earth. That has always been God's desire for a community based on true faith.

You are hardwired for community

MANY OF US WISH that our Christian life could solely depend on our private interactions with God, but English poet John Donne famously reminds us that we are interconnected with the Body:

> No man is an island,
> Entire of itself;
> Every man is a piece of the continent,
> A part of the main.[179]

But as much as some of us introverts and antisocial types would like to live separated from a larger community, it just isn't possible. It never has been and never will be. "Autonomous Christianity never works, because our spiritual life was designed by God to be a community project."[180] One of the first announcements in the Garden of Eden touched on this reality. In Genesis 2, we see an idyllic time described. God created Adam and they were togeth-

[179] John Donne, *No Man is an Island,* 1624
[180] Paul David Tripp, *Dangerous Calling: Confronting the Unique Challenges of Pastoral Ministry*, (Crossway Publishers, 2012), 38.

er, all day, every day. Nothing separated them and they were in a perfect relationship. Yet in the midst of the blissful, spiritual wilderness, God announced, "It is not good that man should be alone."[181] It wasn't enough for Adam to only be with God. So God gave him a helpmate. And the rest is history.

This story of community has continued to be woven through the heart of God's people. Noah, Abraham, and Israel each had aspects of a faith community. Each had differing facets of spiritual growth, prayer, and physical representations of God's presence on earth. It extended through the patriarchs and on through to the firmly established kingdom of David. The psalmist king sang,

> Behold, how good and how pleasant it is
> For brethren to dwell together in unity!
> It is like the precious oil upon the head,
> Running down on the beard,
> The beard of Aaron,
> Running down on the edge of his garments.
> It is like the dew of Hermon,
> Descending upon the mountains of Zion;
> For there the Lord commanded the blessing —
> Life forevermore.[182]

---

[181] Genesis 2:18
[182] Psalm 133

This song moves beyond the need for community to the promises for those who choose to live in a united community of faith, something that commands a literal blessing of life forevermore.

Later, the wise King Solomon pointed to the exponential power of community in Ecclesiastes 4:

> Two are better than one,
> Because they have a good reward for their labor.
> For if they fall, one will lift up his companion.
> But woe to him who is alone when he falls,
> For he has no one to help him up.
> Again, if two lie down together, they will keep warm;
> But how can one be warm alone?
> Though one may be overpowered by another, two can withstand him. And a threefold cord is not quickly broken.[183]

Just look at that exponential growth in action: "Two are better than one" and "a threefold cord is not quickly broken."

This word from Solomon is a wonderful proclamation that foreshadowed the teaching of Jesus to his disciples in Matthew 18:

---

183 Ecclesiastes 4:9-12

> Again I say to you that if two of you agree on earth concerning anything that they ask, it will be done for them by My Father in heaven. For where two or three are gathered together in My name, I am there in the midst of them.[184]

We move to "better together because Jesus is in the middle." It is hard to find a similar biblical promise that is so straightforward and to the point. This need for community was central to Jesus' work with the disciples. It was important enough to collectively overlook Peter's brashness, Thomas's doubt, Judas's shortchanging, Nathanael's judgmental attitude, Matthew's shady connections, James's desire for revenge, Simon the Zealot's revolutionary bent, and John's competitive spirit.

This exponentiality caused by a united faith community was on display after the resurrection and throughout the Book of Acts. In Acts 2 we read:

> When the Day of Pentecost had fully come, they were all with one accord in one place. And suddenly there came a sound from heaven, as of a rushing mighty wind, and it filled the whole house where they were sitting. Then there appeared to them divided tongues, as of fire, and one sat upon each of them. And they were all filled with

---

[184] Matthew 18:19-20

> the Holy Spirit and began to speak with other tongues, as the Spirit gave them utterance.[185]

The original 12 had expanded to include 120, who extended beyond middle-aged men to include women, young men, young ladies, and the elderly. The power of God was poured out on all flesh.

This was not a one-time occurrence quickly shelved for a more private faith journey. Much like Jesus, they continued to meet daily. Continuing in Acts 2:

> So continuing daily with one accord in the temple, and breaking bread from house to house, they ate their food with gladness and simplicity of heart, praising God and having favor with all the people. And the Lord added to the church daily those who were being saved.[186]

The Early Church realized, as Spurgeon did, that some Christians try to go to heaven alone, in solitude. But believers are not compared to bears or lions or other animals that wander alone. Those who belong to Christ are sheep in this respect, that they love to get together. Sheep go in flocks,

---

185 Acts 2:1-47

186 Ibid

and so do God's people.[187] This truth could not be further from our current state of individualistic Christianity.

After the apostle Paul had been knocked off his high horse on the road to Damascus, he quickly found that he had fallen into a Jesus-centered faith community that looked similar to the synagogues he had been a part of his entire life. Yet something was different. Very soon he noticed that every race and gender was represented inside of its sacred space. He saw firsthand what John wrote:

> As many as received Him, to them He gave the right to become children of God, to those who believe in His name: who were born, not of blood, nor of the will of the flesh, nor of the will of man, but of God.[188]

This new community was filled with ethnic, linguistic, cultural, and generational diversity. He saw when Barnabas came looking for him to integrate him into the larger church family, that the doors had been flung open in the kingdom of God due to Jesus' work. As a result, he could confidently write in Galatians 3:26-29:

> For you are all sons of God through faith in Christ Jesus. For as many of you as were baptized into Christ have

---

[187] C. H. Spurgeon from a sermon on Nov. 2, 1884, at Metropolitan Tabernacle, Newington

[188] John 1:12-13

> put on Christ. There is neither Jew nor Greek, there is neither slave nor free, there is neither male nor female; for you are all one in Christ Jesus. And if you are Christ's, then you are Abraham's seed, and heirs according to the promise.

This meant complete equality, all of them now considered children. They would be eligible for their eternal inheritance as opposed to being excluded due to cultural barriers involving gender and race.

In the Epistle to the Hebrews, the Jews, the old synagogue guard that had entered the new community now called the Church, were warned to recognize the tendency to drift from their collective custom:

> Let us hold fast the confession of our hope without wavering, for He who promised is faithful. And let us consider one another in order to stir up love and good works, not forsaking the assembling of ourselves together, as is the manner of some, but exhorting one another, and so much the more as you see the Day approaching.[189]

This passage serves as both an admonition and an encouragement. Are you tired of your community? Make the deci-

---

[189] Hebrews 10:23-25

sion to keep showing up; you won't be disappointed that you did. Can you see the "day approaching"? Then stick with it. God has placed you in your community to help you live the exponential life.

Community leads to true Communion

EVENTUALLY, when we have fully embraced it, wilderness will become our preferred place of spiritual labor, quite possibly rising to the level of an oasis for our soul. It should, as happened in the life of Jesus and his disciples, become the place we long for and strive to enter as frequently as we can. The solitude, silence, and stillness prepare us to step into our community.

Just like bees in a garden, we will float from wilderness flower to wilderness flower, from bloom to blossom, experiencing the ever-deepening profundity of God. Our times of praying, fasting, reading, and listening will center on enjoying our Creator's company. But, like the bee, we cannot live outside of the hive. God created us for wilderness, where we do our deepest spiritual work. Yet he also created in us the need for a faith community.

Whether we admit it or not, we need God. We also have an innate need for someone to care about us. For that reason, Jesus laid out our need for true communion. Between Palm Sunday and Good Friday he invited his disciples to a special Upper Room where they ate their annual Passover meal. When they arrived, the turn of events frightened them. Rather than being a simple potluck evening, it turned into a lesson they were tasked to repeat frequently "in remembrance" of Jesus, their teacher and Savior.

In John 13, just before the beautiful symbolism of the Lord's Supper was instituted, the Master took up the basin and towel, and assumed the position of a servant, much to the surprise and shock of some of his closest friends. He told them why in verses 12-17:

> So when He had washed their feet, taken His garments, and sat down again, He said to them, "Do you know what I have done to you? You call Me Teacher and Lord, and you say well, for so I am. If I then, your Lord and Teacher, have washed your feet, you also ought to wash one another's feet. For I have given you an example, that you should do as I have done to you. Most assuredly, I say to you, a servant is not greater than his master; nor is he who is sent greater than he who sent him. If you know these things, blessed are you if you do them.

What was his reason for doing this? It was the most common of jobs performed by a lowly servant. To their complete surprise, their Master stooped down, humbled himself, and served their most basic needs. It was done so that they would follow his example and, when the occasion afforded them the opportunity, repeat what he had done.

Couple Christ's modeled behavior here with the Lord's Supper and his following proclamation in verses 34-35: "A new commandment I give to you, that you love one another; as I have loved you, that you also love one another. By this all will know that you are My disciples, if you have love for one another." When we take these verses together, we are given a full view of his expectation of his Church. It is a direct reflection of our needs. We need God. We need unconditional love. We need to be needed. We need to humble ourselves so that we can be served. It is all wrapped up in that Upper Room with the broken bread, the basin and the towel, and the new commandment that would lay the foundation for the coming of the Holy Spirit.

Those who are committed to truly entering into a faith community know what South African theologian Desmond Tutu meant when he said, "Like when you sit in front of a fire in winter — you are just there in front of the fire. You don't have to be smart or anything. The fire warms you."[190] You don't have to know all the science behind it. It just happens. When we get together with others, in faith, Jesus is there. That one fact is enough for me to make church attendance a priority. Those on the path to the exponential

[190] Desmond Tutu on NPR's *Morning Edition*, "Insisting We Are 'Made For Goodness" on March 11, 2010.

life will recognize that much more than your church needs you. Community involves serving and being served, loving others, being transparent and confessing failures, forgiving each other's faults, and together receiving what God has promised.

We must realize our need for others. We cannot step into the promise of the exponential life in the wilderness alone. We need other Christians. As author A. W. Tozer explained, this dynamic of a faith community provides a conduit for the Spirit:

> Unity is necessary to the outpouring of the Spirit of God. If you have 120 volts of electricity coming into your house but you have broken wiring, you may turn on the switch, but nothing works — no lights come on, the stove doesn't warm, the radio doesn't turn on. Why? Because you have broken wiring. The power is ready to do its work, but where there is broken wiring, there is no power. Unity is necessary among the children of God if we are going to know the flow of power to see God do His wonders.[191]

We need to study the Word of God together to grow in our spiritual lives. We need to pray together and for each other.

---

[191] A.W. Tozer, *Success and the Christian: The Cost of Spiritual Maturity*, (Wingspread Publication, 2006), 86.

Together we need to make every effort possible to be the physical presence of Jesus here on earth.

Is the Church the Body of Christ or simply a building?

PAUL'S UNDERSTANDING of the Church was profound — maybe unparalleled — in church history. In Romans 12, he writes that by joining the family of God in sonship, we actually become a part of Christ's body:

> For as we have many members in one body, but all the members do not have the same function, so we, being many, are one body in Christ, and individually members of one another. Having then gifts differing according to the grace that is given to us, let us use them.[192]

Again, we are united as a community, but diverse. Our physical body has 78 organs, 206 bones, more than 600 muscles, and somewhere around 37.2 trillion cells — all with different functions, purposes, strengths, and weaknesses. Yet all are an integral part of the body.

Paul says that we are not here to take up space, but that we have a function. We have "gifts" to offer our faith com-

[192] Romans 12:4-6

munity given to us by the grace of God. Some people are intimidated because they think their gift is not as important as someone else's. Maybe it is not visible like others, but it is still vital and needed. Paul addresses this in 1 Corinthians 12:

> But now indeed there are many members, yet one body. And the eye cannot say to the hand, "I have no need of you"; nor again the head to the feet, "I have no need of you." No, much rather, those members of the body which seem to be weaker are necessary. And those members of the body which we think to be less honorable, on these we bestow greater honor; and our unpresentable parts have greater modesty, but our presentable parts have no need. But God composed the body, having given greater honor to that part which lacks it, that there should be no schism in the body, but that the members should have the same care for one another. And if one member suffers, all the members suffer with it; or if one member is honored, all the members rejoice with it. Now you are the body of Christ, and members individually.[193]

Here once again, we see one body, one community, and a lot of diversity.

---

193 1 Corinthians 12:20-26

Our faith community is the primary place God has given us to use our gifts and talents. Martyred Chinese pastor Watchman Nee said:

> The Cross must do its work here, reminding me that in Christ I have died to that old life of independence which I inherited from Adam, and that in resurrection I have become not just an individual believer in Christ but a member of His Body. There is a vast difference between the two. When I see this, I shall at once have done with independence and shall seek fellowship. The life of Christ in me will gravitate to the life of Christ in others. I can no longer take an individual line. Jealousy will go. Competition will go. Private work will go. My interests, my ambitions, my preferences, all will go. It will no longer matter which of us does the work. All that will matter will be that the Body grows.[194]

In this place you realize that your gifts are given by God to serve the body of Christ, and not your own self-promotion. If you are ignorant of your gifts in your faith community, yet are not currently investing them to serve your community, then let yourself hear the voice of God. You have exponentially more to give to your community.

---

[194] Watchman Nee, *The Normal Christian Life*, (Living Stream Ministry, 1992), 130.

It is also important to point out Jesus' distinction between gatherings of people, specifically between a congregation and a crowd. The one he ran to and the other he ran from. The Latin root word for congregation is the verb *congregate,* which literally means "flock with," reminiscent of every time we notice a grouping of birds flying overhead. They are joined together to accomplish a common cause, mainly as a result of their DNA. Something in their identity that tells them to do so. On the other hand, a crowd is a "large number of people gathered together in a disorganized or unruly way." The original sense of the Middle English word is even more revealing. It simply means to "move by pushing."[195]

Eugene Peterson lovingly pointed out the danger of "crowds" when he stated that the level of danger they present to the true spirit of the gospel is on par with "excessive drink and depersonalized sex." He wrote, "A crowd is an exercise in false transcendence upward, which is why all crowds are spiritually pretty much the same, whether at football games, political rallies, or church." He then warns us of becoming a part of something that is altogether wrong when he paraphrased Danish philosopher Søren Kierkegaard's famous assessment of the true nature of crowds: "the more people, the less truth."[196]

---

195 Oxford Dictionary.
196 Eugene Peterson, *The Pastor*, USA, HarperOne, 2012, pg. 157.

Your community needs to be close enough to your daily life to open up opportunities of spiritual correction when needed, as opposed to a once-a-week event where only the most superficial areas are in view. If you are unsure exactly what you are committed to, do a simple assessment of your current community. Ask yourself if you go for the show. If so, then you are most likely committed to a crowd. However, if you go to serve, you can be assured that you belong to a congregation. Follow Jesus' lead on community. Run from the crowds and run toward a real congregation.

Your community will be the place where you live out your faith. Theologian Gordon Fee said, "It is far easier to be a Christian in isolation than it is to live out one's faith in the context of all those other imperfect people that make up God's Church."[197] Pastor Nicky Gumbel of Holy Trinity Brompton in London, tweeted that it only takes a few weekly visits to realize that our "churches are not museums that display perfect people. They are hospitals where the wounded, hurt, injured, and broken find healing."[198] In this atmosphere, we learn to forgive and be forgiven, to listen and be heard, to serve and be served, and to give and receive. It is the place we learn to submit to those God has placed in spiritual authority over us, or, if we are tasked

[197] Gordon Fee, *God's Empowering Presence: The Holy Spirit in the Letters of Paul*, (Baker Academic, 2012) 126.

[198] Gumbel, N [@nicky Gumbel]. (2017, Dec. 4). Twitter. https://twitter.com/nickygumbel/status/937792105388363776 Nicky Gumbel.

with assuming that role, how to humbly lead those under our care.

The Church is the vulnerable soil our lives need to grow in faith. To truly be in community with others means that we make ourselves vulnerable. One cannot be vulnerable alone; an additional party is required. This became real to me when I read the amazing book on community *Life Together,* written by 20th century martyr Dietrich Bonhoeffer. John the Beloved drew attention to the need for others in our life: "If someone says, 'I love God,' and hates his brother, he is a liar; for he who does not love his brother whom he has seen, how can he love God whom he has not seen?"[199] The community is there to teach us to love and because this requires vulnerability, it means there is a risk of being hurt.

Jesus responded to this fear when he answered Peter's question in Matthew 18. "Then Peter came to Him and said, 'Lord, how often shall my brother sin against me, and I forgive him? Up to seven times?' Jesus said to him, "'I do not say to you, up to seven times, but up to seventy times seven.'"[200] Yes, he tells him to forgive, but at its root, Jesus is reminding the disciples to remain vulnerable, and not walk away from their community. If we can persevere even when it hurts, the benefits will far outweigh the pain.

---

[199] 1 John 4:20
[200] Matthew 18:21-35

Our community of faith is a place we should yearn to be in, not begrudgingly attend. It should be the highlight of our week and the place of deepest relationships. English minister John Angell James reminded us, "They who would grow in grace, must love the habitation of God's house. It is those that are planted in the courts of the Lord who shall flourish, and not those that are occasionally there."[201]

Make the commitment to embrace the exponential life and, when you do, you will commit to your faith community. You will look past the shortcomings of others and see their place in your process. You will find your place of greatest service and your gifts will blossom. You will become more like Jesus, who himself had to put up with the shortcomings of his community. But he never gave up his regular observance. You must realize you are not committing to a perfect community, but rather an imperfect one, one that is striving to be perfected by Jesus. The idea of the perfect church is a red herring, as Spurgeon explained, "If I had never joined a church till I had found one that was perfect, I should never have joined one at all. And the moment I did join it, if I had found one, I should have spoiled it, for it would not have been a perfect church after I had become

---

[201] Josiah Hotchkiss Gilbert, *Dictionary of Burning Words of Brilliant Writers: A Cyclopædia of Quotations from the Literature of All Ages*, (W.B. Ketcham, 1895), 150.

a member of it. Still, imperfect as it is, it is the dearest place on earth to us!"[202]

Make it personal

1. What would you consider the hallmarks of the perfect church? Do you find these qualities in yourself?

2. Do you have someone you look to as a mentor that you respect enough to allow him or her to speak difficult truths to you? Does someone look to you in this capacity?

3. What contribution can/do you make to your church community?

[202] Quote found in Charles Spurgeon's sermon entitled, "The Best Donation" (No. 2234), an exposition of 2 Corinthians 8:5 delivered on April 5, 1891 at the Metropolitan Tabernacle in London, England.

Paradoxical Imperatives for Relating to Self

8. On-Ramp of Self-Denial

I HAVE LEARNED more about my spiritual life from my four kids than any book I have ever read on the subject. It started the moment I held my firstborn in my arms and fell in love with being a father. It gave me so much insight into my Heavenly Father's love toward us. My failures have helped me to give less advice about things I don't know by way of personal experience and to be sympathetic with those who are suffering through their current realities. It has also taught me that no one likes to hear "no" in response to a desired request.

This lesson became very clear when our two oldest were in their infancy, 2 and 3 years old. The older, taking his place as the spokesperson for the two — because his brother couldn't yet put together a sentence — had asked to do something suspect. My answer was a resounding "no." He then turned around in frustration and mumbled under his breath, "You don't let us do nothing." His younger brother, not quite able to fully express his disappointment verbally, darted his eyes toward me and simply said "nuffin!" Even though his linguist capabilities didn't yet allow him full expression, his one jumbled response spoke volumes. How well do you receive the "no" when it comes from someone else? This is reality. How about when it comes from yourself? This is self-discipline. How about when it comes from God? This is spiritual maturity.

Anytime we ask someone, even God, a "yes or no" petition, we must understand that at best it is a 50/50 proposition. Many Christians claim the God they serve is a "yes-only" God. They have allowed the modern American mentality of consumerism to impact their understanding of God. They believe that they — the customer — are always right and that God, the celestial customer service manager, should do whatever is demanded to make things right. The phenomenon is disturbingly prevalent and is rooted in moral therapeutic deism. If you can only see God as a means to reach your ultimate goal of superficial happiness, then you are not serving God. He isn't our employee.

If you struggle as so many do in our selfish, self-satisfying world with accepting "no" as a valid answer from others, from yourself, and especially from God, then Jesus laid a path for you to follow. He told us in Matthew 16:

> If anyone desires to come after Me, let him deny himself, and take up his cross, and follow Me. For whoever desires to save his life will lose it, but whoever loses his life for My sake will find it. For what profit is it to a man if he gains the whole world, and loses his own soul? Or what will a man give in exchange for his soul?[203]

---

[203] Matthew 16:24-26

This concise and clear concept of denying yourself is a core value for Jesus' disciples, then and now.

A denial of self is the first step in a true relationship with Jesus. "We can learn what it means to deny oneself if we understand what it means to deny another...we act as if he is a stranger to us."[204] We treat him as though he were non-existent or at least nonessential, to our decision-making process. As Scottish evangelist Henry Drummond wrote, "The entrance fee into the kingdom of heaven is nothing: the annual subscription is everything."[205] This step of self-denial is one that must be taken constantly.

Jesus Christ demands self-denial as a necessary condition of discipleship.[206] Self-denial is a summons to submit to the authority of God as Father and of Jesus as Lord and to declare lifelong war on one's instinctive egotism. What we negate is not personality or one's existence as a rational and responsible human being. Jesus does not plan to turn us into zombies, nor does he ask us to volunteer for a robot role. The required denial is of the carnal self: the egocentric, self-deifying urge that dominates us so ruinously in our natural state.

---

[204] Theophylact of Ochrid, *The Explanation*, USA, (Chrysostom Press, 1992), 70.

[205] William MacDonald, *The Believer's Bible Commentary,* (Thomas Nelson, 2008), 1428.

[206] Matthew 16:24; Mark 8:34; Luke 9:23

The Lord links self-denial with cross-bearing. Cross-bearing is far more than enduring hardship. Carrying one's cross in Jesus' day, as we learn from Jesus' own crucifixion, was required of those whom society had condemned, whose rights were forfeited, and who trudged to their own execution. The cross they carried was an instrument of death. Jesus represents discipleship as a matter of following him, based on taking up one's cross in self-negation. Carnal self never consents to being cast in such a role. "When Christ calls a man, he bids him come and die," wrote Dietrich Bonhoeffer.[207] Many years later J. I. Packer observed this on-ramp. "Bonhoeffer was right: Accepting death to everything that the carnal self wants to possess is what Christ's summons to self-denial was all about."[208]

These verses, central to Jesus' calling of his disciples, are not popular these days. But self-centered faith is nothing new. Puritan Richard Baxter wrote about this nearly 400 years ago:

> Naturally, men are prone to spin themselves a web of opinions out of their own brain, and to have a religion that may be called their own. They are far readier to make themselves a faith, than to receive that which God

---

[207]Dietrich Bonhoeffer, *The Cost of Discipleship* (Touchstone, 1995), 89.

[208] J.I. Packer, *Hot Tub Religion*, (Living Books, Tyndale House,1987), 72-73.

> hath formed to their hands; are far readier to receive a doctrine that tends to their carnal commodity, or honor, or delight, than one that tends to self-denial.[209]

Our selfishness is like a river, looking for the path of least resistance in its trek to the lowest point. For that reason, many have overlooked or ignored the need of self-denial as an important imperative that leads to the exponential life. Many think the full, abundant, overflowing, exponential life that Jesus promised his disciples was all about getting others to say "yes," or about idolizing your personal happiness by always saying "yes" to yourself, and of course God should get on board with a "yes." A man-made God always sounds oddly like the man who made him.

True relationship with God looks completely different. English minister Matthew Henry wrote, "The first lesson in Christ's school is self-denial."[210] If we have not learned that lesson, maybe we need to reevaluate and listen more intently to God's voice. Let us reach the conviction that, "If our life is not a course of humility, self-denial, renunciation of the world, poverty of spirit, and heavenly affection, we do

---

[209] *A Dictionary of Thoughts: Being a Cyclopedia of Laconic Quotations from the Best Authors, Both Ancient and Modern*, (Cassell Publishing Co. 1891), 165.

[210] Matthew Henry, *Dictionary of Burning Words of Brilliant Writers*, (1895), 535.

not live the lives of Christians."[211] Avoiding self-denial can become a stumbling block to obedience. I even encourage you to adopt the attitude shared by Indian missionary Sandu Sundar Singh:

> Those who determine not to put self to death will never see the will of God fulfilled in their lives. Those who ought to become the light of the world must necessarily burn and become less and less. By denying self, we are able to win others.[212]

Singh put this truth to song when he captured the dying words of Indian martyr Nokseng in the classic hymn, "I Have Decided to Follow Jesus."[213]

The apostle Paul wrote from this place of self-denial when he famously confessed that he had "been crucified with Christ." "It is no longer I who live," he continued, "but Christ lives in me; and the life which I now live in the flesh I live by faith in the Son of God, who loved me and gave Himself for me."[214] Any attempts at vague duplicity concerning who is calling the shots will place you on a dangerous crash course. Author Elisabeth Elliot explains the

---

[211] William Law, *A Serious Call to a Devout and Holy Life,* (Hendrickson Publishers, 2009), 6.

[212] W.K. Volkmer, *These Things: A Reference Manual for Discipleship*, (Lulu.com), 203.

[213] Sandu Sundar Singh, *I Have Decided to Follow Jesus,* 19th Century

[214] Galatians 2:20

collision like this: "When the will of God crosses the will of man, somebody has to die."[215] Revivalist Jonathan Edwards agreed with Jesus and Paul on this when he explained that it is not in telling people about ourselves that we demonstrate our Christianity because "words are cheap, and godliness is more easily feigned in words than in actions. Christian practice is a costly laborious thing. The self-denial that is required of Christians, the narrowness of the way that leads to life, does not consist in words, but in practice."[216]

Getting yourself out of your way

In Shakespeare's *Hamlet*, Polonius famously proclaims, "to thine own self be true."[217] This phrase has been repurposed these days to mean that you allow yourself to become the center of your universe, even to the point of becoming the infallible center of your universe. In that same vein, we casually tell our kids to "follow your heart." This is a damaging, yet common path to take and characterizes our age of selfish ambition and narcissism.

---

[215] Elisabeth Elliot, *Passion and Purity: Learning to Bring Your Love Life Under Christ's Control*, (Fleming H. Revell, 2012), 72.

[216] Jonathan Edwards, *The Complete Works of Jonathan Edwards*, (Samizdat Express, 1834), 2812.

[217] William Shakespeare, *Hamlet*, (1623), Act I, Scene 3

For a disciple of Christ, it is not only damaging, but also leads us to a place of idolatry in the form of self-worship. It only takes a few sacred pauses to hear that our self doesn't belong in the place reserved solely for God.

The prophet Jeremiah spells it out in the 17th chapter of the book bearing his name:

> The heart is deceitful above all things,
> And desperately wicked;
> Who can know it?
> I, the Lord, search the heart,
> I test the mind,
> Even to give every man according to his ways,
> According to the fruit of his doings.[218]

And in the Proverbs of Solomon we read in 28:26, "He that trusts his own heart is a fool." Again, in Matthew 15:19,[219] Jesus made it clear how untrustworthy our self can be when he said, "For from the heart come evil thoughts, murder, adultery, all sexual immorality, theft, lying, and slander."

You may look in the mirror and say, "There is no way that I am that bad. I am not like a murderer or a thief." The reality is you are most likely worse. Matthew Henry explains:

---

[218] Jeremiah 17:9-10
[219] NIV

There is that wickedness in our hearts which we ourselves are not aware of and do not suspect to be there; nay, it is a common mistake among the children of men to think themselves, their own hearts at least, a great deal better than they really are. The heart, the conscience of man, in his corrupt and fallen state, is deceitful above all things. It is subtle and false; it is apt to supplant (so the word properly signifies); it is that from which Jacob had his name, a supplanter. It calls evil good and good evil, puts false colours upon things, and cries peace to those to whom peace does not belong.
When men say in their hearts (that is, suffer their hearts to whisper to them) that there is no God, or he does not see, or he will not require, or they shall have peace though they go on; in these, and a thousand similar suggestions the heart is deceitful. It cheats men into their own ruin; and this will be the aggravation of it, that they are self-deceivers, self-destroyers. Herein the heart is desperately wicked; it is deadly, it is desperate. The case is bad indeed, and in a manner deplorable and past relief, if the conscience which should rectify the errors of the other faculties is itself a mother of falsehood and a ring-leader in the delusion. What will become of a man if that in him which should be the candle of the Lord give a false light, if God's deputy in the soul, that is entrusted to support his interests, betrays them? Such is the deceitfulness of the heart that we may truly say, Who

> can know it? Who can describe how bad the heart is? We cannot know our own hearts, not what they will do in an hour of temptation (Hezekiah did not, Peter did not), not what corrupt dispositions there are in them, nor in how many things they have turned aside; who can understand his errors? Much less can we know the hearts of others, or have any dependence upon them.[220]

For Christ's disciples, it is discouraging that we have made such an untrustworthy companion the center of our lives, our churches, and our communities.

Once we realize this cancer of self has metastasized into every corner of our existence and is destroying our real self — that created in the image of God — we must act to overcome it. But like a malignant tumor, the carnal self is not easily extricated once it has taken root. Richard Baxter once again gave us a reality check when he wrote, "Self is the most treacherous enemy, and the most insinuating deceiver in the world. Of all other vices, it is both the hardest to find out, and the hardest to cure."[221] But cure it we must, if only by the grace of God.

---

[220] Matthew Henry, *Matthew Henry's Commentary on the Whole Bible: Volume IV-II - Jeremiah to Lamentations*, (Devoted Publishing, 2017), 115.

[221] Richard Baxter, *The Practical Works of Richard Baxter*, (J Duncan, 1830), 119.

The pry bar of self-denial is fasting

ABSTINENCE OR FASTING reminds us of our need to listen in our process of becoming fruitful. It is the realization that each time I say "yes" to one thing, it means saying "no" to something else. As a result, fasting in its simplest form is saying "no" to something primal, so that we can say "yes" to something eternal in our pursuit of God. According to psychologist Abraham Maslow's pyramid theory, we all have the same basic needs: food, water, warmth, and rest. Fasting is simply telling one of my basic needs "no." It is telling my inner wants and needs "no" while telling God "yes." As Dallas Willard wrote, "Fasting confirms our utter dependence upon God by finding in Him a source of sustenance beyond food."[222]

Jesus spoke clearly to his disciples about his expectation that they would fast, just as he did during his 40 days in the desert. He also brought to light the power that accompanied them when they said "no" to their desires. In Matthew 6:16-18, we are reminded when he begins his instruction by saying not "if" but "when." This was not an option to be negotiated by his followers. He continues with a clear direction:

---

[222] Dallas Willard, *The Spirit of the Disciplines*, (Harper One, 1999), 166.

> Moreover, when you fast, do not be like the hypocrites, with a sad countenance. For they disfigure their faces that they may appear to men to be fasting. Assuredly, I say to you, they have their reward. But you, when you fast, anoint your head and wash your face, so that you do not appear to men to be fasting, but to your Father who is in the secret place; and your Father who sees in secret will reward you openly.

He let us know that we do not fast for the approval of others, so that they may think we are on a higher plane spiritually from everyone else. We do it to pursue God. We do it to quiet the busyness and noise of our lives. We do it so that we can lean in, listen, and ultimately hear God's voice.

Fasting extends much further than our basic needs of food and water. It can also extend to any activity we spend our precious time doing. It can include our leisure time, our vacation time, our meal time. At one point in my life, I felt compelled to fast from watching sports on television so that I could spend that time pursuing God. I remember the first Saturday that I did not watch or listen to my favorite college team's game. My wife was astonished that after almost 20 years of habitual participation in this pastime, I gave it up, for no other reason than to pursue God. It didn't affect the outcome of the game, but it did affect me. Scottish minister Andrew Bonar points to this broad understanding of abstinence or denying self when he explained, "Fasting is abstaining from anything that hinders prayer."[223]

John Cassian explained the realistic nature of the varieties of fasting so well when instructing his monastic brethren. He wrote:

> Let us not believe that an external fast from visible food alone can possibly be sufficient for perfection of heart and purity of body unless with it there has also been united a fast of the soul. For the soul also has its foods that are harmful. Slander is its food and indeed one that is very dear to it. A burst of anger also supplies it with miserable food for an hour and destroys it as well with its deadly savor. Envy is food of the mind, corrupting it with its poisonous juices and never ceasing to make it wretched and miserable at the prosperity and success of another. Vanity is its food which gratifies the mind with a delicious meal for a time but afterward strips it clear and bare of all virtue. Then vanity dismisses it barren and void of all spiritual fruit. All lust and shift wanderings of heart are a sort of food for the soul, nourishing it on harmful meats but leaving it afterwards without a share of its heavenly bread and really solid food. If then, with all the powers we have, we abstain from these in a

[223]Wendy Speake, *The 40-Day Sugar Fast: Where Physical Detox Meets Spiritual Transformation,* (Baker Publishing, 2019) 89.

> most holy fast our observance of the bodily fast will be both useful and profitable.[224]

We all have something, a particular habit or vice we can lay down in our pursuit of a deeper relationship with God.

British evangelist Roy Hession expounds on Cassian's sentiments and takes us a bit further:

> Dying to self is not a thing we do once for all. There may be an initial dying when God first shows these things, but ever after it will be a constant dying, for only so can the Lord Jesus be revealed constantly through us. All day long the choice will be before us in a thousand ways. It will mean no plans, no time, no money, no pleasure of our own. It will mean a constant yielding to those around us, for our yieldedness to God is measured by our yieldedness to man. Every humiliation, everyone who tries and vexes us, is God's way of breaking us, so that there is a yet deeper channel in us for the Life of Christ.[225]

Rather than being a somber and life-draining discipline, he sums it up like this:

---

[224] John Cassian, *Nicene and Post Nicene Fathers,* Ed. Philip Schaff, Series II, Vol. 11, Chapter XXI.

[225] Roy Hession, *My Calvary Road*, (CLC Publications, 2011), 154.

> People imagine that dying to self makes one miserable. But it is just the opposite. It is the refusal to die to self that makes one miserable. The more we know of death with Him, the more we shall know of His life in us, and so the more of real peace and joy.[226]

I agree completely! Each time I make the effort to fast, whether food or leisure, I have seen the benefits.

It seems that God has so much more that he wants to give me, but my hands are always full. Andrew Murray saw this connection. "Prayer," he wrote, "is reaching out for God and the unseen; fasting is letting go of all that is seen and temporal. Fasting helps express, deepen, confirm the resolution that we are ready to sacrifice anything, even ourselves to attain what we seek for the kingdom of God."[227] Fasting allows me to let go of something, even if it's only long enough to allow him to give me what he wants me to have. This reality is reflected in Jesus' promise that those who fast can be certain that "your Father who sees in secret will reward you openly."[228]

Most of us who hate to hear "no" as an answer to our petitions also cringe when we have to tell someone else "no" when they ask something of us. This causes us to build

---

[226] Rebecca English, Living the Christ Life: A collection of Daily Readings by Classic Deeper-Life Authors, (CLC, 2009), 21.

[227] Andrew Murray, *The Andrew Murray on Collection*, (Karpathos Collections), 2385.

[228] Matthew 6:18

an idol of acceptance alongside the one of self. We do this day in and day out, and consequently we find ourselves full of anxiety because we have sacrificed half of our ability to give a perfectly valid answer to the request of another person. Each time we do we are bowing down before that idol in worship. I have seen the fruit of this idolatry in frustrated friends, temperamental teenagers, exhausted parents, miserable workers, and emotionally dead disciples. All because they will not become their true self through fasting. "Until you have given up your 'self' to Him you will not have a real 'self.'"[229] Fasting is where we give up our right to be right and our desire to please others. It is there that we commit to perform for an audience of One.

A real benefit of biblical fasting is to find joy in saying "no" to ourselves, as well as learning that what we tell ourselves we want may not be what we actually need. This also frees us within our relationship with others. If we learn the beauty of "no" as a valid answer to ourselves, it will empower us to be ready to give it to others. We will never be able to utter "no" as a valid response to those who are asking for our time, unless we learn to speak it to ourselves.

Jesus admitted to his disciples that fasting does change our situation in ways that otherwise would remain unchanged when he taught them concerning a spiritual battle involving a demon in Matthew 17:21. He said, "However,

---

[229] C.S. Lewis, *Mere Christianity* (Touchstone, 1996), 190-191.

this kind does not go out except by prayer and fasting." In my process to become fruitful, I must remind myself that fasting has more to do with the transformation of my being than the enhancement of my asking power. There is a supernatural leverage that seems to be a common benefit of those who fast. Augustine wrote, "Fasting cleanses the soul, raises the mind, subjects one's flesh to the spirit, renders the heart contrite and humble, scatters the clouds of concupiscence, quenches the fire of lust, and kindles the true light of chastity. Enter again into yourself."[230] Fasting simply gets me out of my own way.

Lest we fall into error

WHEN WE TALK about fasting, it is easy to allow your mind to drift to the extremes that we have encountered or read about in our spiritual journey. We might imagine those who pledge to personally fast for a political reason until there is a change. They are committed to their purpose, even to the point of death. This is much less like a fast than a hunger strike. Others do intermittent fasting for weight loss, which resembles dieting more closely than what Jesus spoke about. While admirable, this is not biblical fast-

[230] Jonathan Munn, *Anglican Catholicism: Unchanging Faith in a Changing World*, (Lulu, 2019), 360.

ing. Fasting is nothing if it isn't focused on getting myself out of the way, so that I might draw nearer to God. Conditioning yourself to realize that "no" is not a dirty word or taboo, but a constant reality in the deeper life, will only better prepare us to accept it more generously when it comes from Our Heavenly Father's lips.

Yet as powerful as self-denial seems, it cannot stand alone. It must be coupled with prayer. As Matthew Henry noted,

> If the solemnities of our fasting, though frequent, long, and severe, do not serve to put an edge upon devout affections, to quicken prayer, to increase Godly sorrow, and to alter the temper of our minds, and the course of our lives, for the better, they do not at all answer the intention, and God will not accept them as performed to Him.[231]

If the spiritual discipline of saying "no" is separated from prayer, it ceases to be a fast and should simply be called nothing more than a diet or an act of the will. As Church father Ignatius realized, "Few souls understand what God would accomplish in them if they were to abandon them-

---

[231] Matthew Henry, *Matthew Henry's Commentary on the Whole Bible: Volume 2*, (Joseph Ogle Robinson, UK, 1828), 1478.

selves unreservedly to Him and if they were to allow His grace to mold them accordingly."[232]

Self-denial leads to self-control. In Romans 12:1-2, Paul states that this act of laying down our selfish desires is like a sacrifice:

> I beseech you therefore, brethren, by the mercies of God, that you present your bodies a living sacrifice, holy, acceptable to God, which is your reasonable service. And do not be conformed to this world, but be transformed by the renewing of your mind, that you may prove what is that good and acceptable and perfect will of God.[233]

Only when I learn to say "no" to myself will I be able to fully say "yes" to God. If we know that the aim of the Holy Spirit is to lead people to the place of self-control, we shall not fall into passivity, but we shall make progress in the spiritual life. The fruit of the Spirit is self-control. I pray that you are convinced to take on fasting in one form or another as a part of your Christian life. You can be certain that what is done in the dark and secret place of your life will find the light of day in its reward from your Father.

---

232 Randy Hain, *Along the Way: Lessons for an Authentic Journey of Faith*, (Liguori, 2012), 144.

233 KJV

Make it personal

1. What takes your attention away from God most often?

2. Reexamine your average daily activity. Are your efforts spent more in the service of yourself or the kingdom of God?

3. Do your actions suggest an attempt to gain the favor of those around you or your Father in Heaven?

4. Have you ever negotiated obedience with God?

9. On-Ramp of Sabbath

I REMEMBER THE DAY when a friend offhandedly revealed to me that I was not respecting the Ten Commandments nearly as much as I supposed. It happened at a training session for missionaries I helped lead. My incredible wife, co-laborer, and partner in ministry and life set up a mini intervention.

Leah had watched my pace of life while fully engaged in planting new churches, training new pastors, mentoring missionaries, as well as inside our house behind closed doors. It was torrid, but I felt fulfilled, indispensable, extremely important, and constantly hurried. The voices raged in my head telling me every day, *If you don't do this, then it will not get done.* This *needed to be done yesterday*, and *You are the only one that can do this.* On and on it went. I would rise early, work hard all day in the ministry, come home, and crash. I hit repeat on that playlist for over four years without one day off: no vacations, no rest days, and no healing.

At the conclusion of an amazing week of training dozens of missionaries, a missionary director named Jay told me he had a question. He is a friend and mentor. He had always encouraged me in my hamster wheel of life. Unbeknownst to me, my loving wife had told Jay of my pace, of the drive to succeed — a drive that, even when wrapped in Jesus jargon, was never healthy or necessary. As we sat in the jungle together, he asked me "Do you believe the Ten Commandments are important for us today?"

I know the look on my face must have revealed that I had no clue why a person who knew completely well that I was a high performer and high producer for the kingdom of God, would ask me a simple Sunday School question. I told him the obvious answer, "yes."

He set me up by asking the follow-up question: "Do you follow the Ten Commandments as rules for your life?" I felt a trap coming, so I quickly scrolled through the big ones that came to my mind. I had never come close to murdering someone. I didn't lie. I didn't steal. I didn't cheat on my wife. I didn't worship other gods. So I again told him, "yes."

Then my dear friend and trusted mentor looked at me with the love of a father and in his sweetest Southern drawl said, "You are lying like a rug."

I was shocked at his directness. I again ran the scroll in my mind, trying to recall any possible act that could constitute a moral failure, but came up with nothing. I asked him what he meant. And he went on to explain that Leah had in fact spilled the beans: I was not taking the Sabbath seriously. He gave me a prescription of mandated rest each week and one extended rest each year.

Just a few weeks later, we took a mini-sabbatical for two weeks. It took me days to unwind and to disengage from the hustle and bustle. It took me over a week to see just how bad things had become and to start to see a way forward. I had grown so accustomed to the grind and hurry. I found myself lost for actions and words. In the middle of the de-programming, I found God, my family, and myself again. I realized that I was too close to everything that I felt needed my attention.

I didn't have enough space between myself and the church, our nonprofit, our Bible school, and the day-in and day-out operations to see the full panorama. It seemed like I was trying to watch a football game while staring at a blade of grass at the 50-yard line while on my knees. After a few days, I started to see the reality more clearly and how to improve the situation. In one fell swoop, Jay had yanked the rug out from under me and turned my world upside down, or more accurately, right side up. From that day of intervention until now, Sabbath has become an essential element of my life.

What exactly are we talking about?

IT ALL STARTED with God's example modeled to his creation in Genesis 2:2 where we are told that, upon completing all his work, he rested on the seventh day. Now anyone with a pulse in theology knows that God doesn't get tired in the human sense of the word. So why would he need to rest? For the sole purpose of giving us an example to follow. He knew that we needed a strongly modeled example of what he was referring to when he wrote with his own finger the fourth of the Ten Commandments. In Exodus 20, he ordered Israel to "Remember the Sabbath day by keeping it holy."[234] This order rather quickly was followed up by the clarifying reminder in Leviticus 23 which expounds, "There are six days when you may work, but the seventh day is a day of sabbath rest, a day of sacred assembly. You are not to do any work; wherever you live, it is a sabbath to the LORD."[235] The directive clearly points back to the opening of Genesis, reminding us that it means to rest, worship, and to disengage from work.

This order to rest and recover was not only intended for humans, but also for the land over which he had given them dominion. In Leviticus 25, we observe another decree:

> When you come into the land which I give you, then the land shall keep a sabbath to the Lord. Six years you shall sow your field, and six years you shall prune your vineyard, and gather its fruit; but in the seventh year there shall be a sabbath of solemn rest for the land, a sabbath to the Lord.[236]

---

[234] NIV
[235] NIV
[236] Leviticus 25:2-4, ESV

Again, we see the phrase "a Sabbath to the Lord." This simple act of obedience in choosing to rest and letting the land rest was an act of worship to God. Yet the act became misconstrued and twisted rather quickly.

The Jews frequently added to the list of things that were not allowed on Sabbath. They overreached to the point of forming special "religious brigades" of rabbis that patrolled to ensure conformity. They spied into homes to ensure no one was cooking, cleaning, starting a fire, lighting candles, combing their hair, or anything else that resembled work. These offenders would be confronted, humiliated, punished adequately, and made to conform immediately. The act of worship for God quickly became a dead obligation to keep God happy, to avoid anything that could possibly tick him off. With that mindset, the Sabbath — a day of rest and a sacred act of worship — became a chore.

As I mentioned in the chapter on community, Jesus honored the Sabbath. Yet Jesus was criticized for healing the sick, for picking grain to eat, and for other minor infractions by the "religious brigade." Their pettiness is revealed when his accusers asked him if it was OK to do "good on the Sabbath." They had so contorted their rules that a man was permitted to help a farm animal in distress, but not another human in despair.

In Matthew 12:12, he rebuked them with a question and its obvious answer, "Of how much more value then is a man than a sheep? Therefore it is lawful to do good on the Sabbath." On another occasion we find Jesus and his famished disciples picking handfuls of wheat to eat on the Sabbath, again upsetting the man-made exaggerations of God's rules. He set things right as Mark 2:27 records, "The Sabbath was made for man, not man for the Sabbath." That, much like the moment of my intervention, turned everything right side up. Jesus reminds us that the commandment is not a chore, but a privilege and a necessity.

Paul gets in on the Sabbath conversation in Romans 14:5. The Jews tried to focus on a particular day of the week and began browbeating others into submission. The apostle clarifies that it isn't a particular day that is sacred; it is the act of worship that is sacred. He stated, "One person considers one day more sacred than another; another considers every day alike. Each of them should be fully convinced in their own mind." It can be Saturday, Sunday, or Thursday for that matter. The sacredness is in the *act*, not the day.

The author of Hebrews helps us realize that the promise of Sabbath is still alive and well for those who look to live the exponential life:

> Therefore, since the promise of entering his rest still stands, let us be careful that none of you be found to have fallen short of it... There remains, then, a Sabbath-rest for the people of God; for anyone who enters God's

> rest also rests from their works, just as God did from his. Let us, therefore, make every effort to enter that rest.[237]

You do it for yourself. You allow yourself to rest, to recover, to refocus, to refresh, to resolve, and to revive. Jesus said that the Sabbath is all about you. It was made for you. Its sole function is your well-being.

Sabbath is a sacred idleness

IT IS CLEAR that we must embrace a Sabbath rest or as Scottish minister George MacDonald called it, a "sacred idleness."[238] Would any of us complain about a car breaking down if we had driven it 300,000 miles without taking it in for maintenance? Of course not. We would probably be giddy that it made it past 50,000 miles without exploding. No one in his right mind would ever do that to a car. Most who make the large investment in a vehicle will follow the stated guidelines for use and maintenance.

Yet few of us are willing to do the same when it comes to Sabbath rest, simply because we never learn to say "no" to all that is vying for our attention. We see from the beginning that this time of sacred idleness was meant to be a

---

237 Hebrews 4:1-11, NIV

238 George MacDonald, *Wilfrid Cumbermede*, (Johannesen Printing and Publishing, 1997), 170.

pause from work, implemented into God's service manual for humans because we truly need to rest. As theologian Walter Bruggemann shows us, "Sabbath, in the first instance, is not about worship. It is about work stoppage. It is about withdrawal from the anxiety system of Pharaoh, the refusal to let one's life be defined by production and consumption and the endless pursuit of private well-being."[239]

Most of our lives are filled with disorder simply due to our refusal to obey when it comes to this point of sacred idleness. We spend six days a week putting knots in our rope and God gives us the one day we need to get them all out. If you go one week without taking the knots out, you can possibly make it up. If you go a month it's a lot more difficult. Some of us go a year or, in my case, many years without stopping to rest. Is it any wonder there is such disarray and dysfunction in our life?

Those who learn to deny themselves and say "no" to all that pulls on them will understand rather quickly the words of the prophet Isaiah recorded in 40:31, "But those who wait on the Lord, Shall renew their strength; They shall mount up with wings like eagles, They shall run and not be weary, They shall walk and not faint." In its simplest form, Sabbath is trusting God enough to obey him, because you believe he knows what you need more than you do. We do this rather than obeying the numerous voices yelling in

---

[239] Walter Bruggemann, *Journey to the Common Good*, (Westminster John Knox Press, 2010), 26.

our head, telling us if we stop the world will end. This decision will lead us to a more fruitful and exponential spiritual life. Brueggeman gives us a glimpse of what can be: "Sabbath is not simply the pause that refreshes. It is the pause that transforms."[240]

This sacred act has a goal: bringing ourselves into full submission to God, resting our bodies, and refocusing on our divine purpose of becoming fruitful. Due to our lack of a true day of sabbath rest, we cannot see all that God is doing. Sabbath breaks the zombie-like trance we live in from day to day. Dulled by the message and the noise of our world and jaded by 24-hour news cycles, we slide into the current and mindlessly trudge along with our non-Christian neighbors. Sabbath reminds us that we are strangers and not of this world. We are called to march to the beat of a different drummer, to be in the world, but not of the world.

Eugene Peterson understood sacred idleness as a time of recognizing that God is in control and seeing all that he is up to in our busy lives. He wrote, "Sabbath is that uncluttered time and space in which we can distance ourselves from our own activities enough to see what God is doing."[241] Looking at the sacred actions will reveal a common thread of listening to what God is saying and doing in our lives.

---

[240] ibid.

[241] Eugene Peterson, *Working the Angles: the Shape of Pastoral Integrity*, (Eerdmans Publishing, 1989), 84.

Sabbath is not leisure

IN THE WESTERN WORLD, we excel in leisure and entertainment, but we fail at rest. This is a symptom that comes from lack of obedience. Our bodies, our minds, and our souls are aching under the constant strain. Martin Luther taught, "The spiritual rest, which God particularly intends in this Commandment, is this: that we not only cease from our labor and trade, but much more, that we let God alone work in us and that we do nothing of our own with all our powers."[242] God has given us the way to heal our overstrained selves through the sacred idleness of Sabbath.

Instead, we consistently buy the lie that we do not need to rest or that somehow we cannot afford to commit to rest. We believe that somehow in being obedient to God we will fall into laziness or maybe others will see it as selfishness. When we reject healing, we are left to sedate our pain through leisure and entertainment. Like morphine offered to a patient who — though not currently terminal — refuses to take time to heal his wounds and chooses to press on at all costs. Sabbath serves as a hospital for healing our body, mind, and soul. Leisure and entertainment are nothing more than an ever-increasing dose of pain-killing drugs.

---

[242] Martin Luther, *Martin Luther Premium Collection: Theological Works, Sermons & Hymns,* (e-artnow, 2018), 858.

The evidence of this is obvious when we look at our days off or free time. They are usually busier than our workdays. Our workdays are so poorly managed that we rarely find rest. There is simply too much to do, too many people depending on us, too many deadlines to meet. In our current state of freedom, we must come to realize as Swiss theologian Karl Barth wrote, "A being is free only when it can determine and limit its activity."[243] God commands us to rest, completely unplug from the world, and remind ourselves that we are not God and the world doesn't stop when we do. Writer Wendall Berry understood this when he wrote, "Sabbath observance invites us to stop. It invites us to rest. It asks us to notice that while we rest, the world continues without our help. It invites us to delight in the world's beauty and abundance."[244]

I have come to share a similar understanding of the paradoxical imperative of Sabbath with Eugene Peterson when he stated, "If you don't take a Sabbath, something is wrong. You're doing too much, you're being too much in charge. You've got to quit, one day a week, and just watch what God is doing when you're not doing anything."[245] The only reason I began practicing sabbath was due to a loving con-

---

243 Ben Witherington III, *Work: A Kingdom Perspective on Labor*, (Eerdmans, 2011), 143.

244 Norma Wirzba, *Living the Sabbath*, (Baker Publishing, 2006), 12.

245 Eugene Peterson, *Working the Angles: the Shape of Pastoral Integrity*, (Eerdmans Publishing, 1989), 84.

frontation from my wife via my friend Jay, who pointed out that I had not had a day of rest for over four years. Although I had taken several days for leisure pursuit, I always remained "on the job." At Leah's urging, I learned that the power of complete rest from only one day is nothing less than supernatural.

Of all the sacred habits this is the one that has been my greatest challenge: learning to say "no" to my selfish desire to be important and needed, and "no" to the requests of others. At the same time, it is the one that has produced the greatest spiritual gains in my life. These on-ramps are all going to the same destination: the exponential life that Jesus promised. You can see that many are interconnected or appear to overlap. I have found that Sabbath is the only one that interconnects with all the others.

These experiences include those singular days when I unplug my computer and make the commitment to not watch television or answer my phone; when I choose to trust God rather than my internal voice that tries to convince me that I don't have the time to sleep in or take a long nap; when I allow the pause that my body needs to recover and that my soul needs. Those are the days when the knots in my rope are undone.

Do you feel like you can make it a few more days without shutting down and truly resting? Do you think that God has made an exception for you inside of his command to rest? Do you trust God more than you trust yourself? More than the busy voices in your head? Do you trust him enough to simply obey?

Where can I start?

START BY TAKING a short nap. Most of us are so tightly wound that we have a hard time really resting. Some have reached the point of needing medicine — both natural and unnatural — to aid in getting the quality sleep they need. One of my favorite examples of this paradoxical imperative is from John Stott, whose days were filled with speaking engagements, writing books, and pastoring churches in England. He lived until 90, full of life and always refreshed.

His secret was to schedule into his daily regimen a sacred space for rest. He called it his HHH or "horizontal half-hour." Sometimes the most Christ-like thing that you can do is to take a nap. It means you recognize that the world will not end simply because you need to rest. If you cannot fit a "horizontal half-hour"[246] into your schedule, then plan a day to just turn off the alarm clock and sleep until you cannot sleep anymore. Either way, just rest.

---

[246] Roger Steer, *Basic Christian: The Inside Story of John Stott*, (InterVarsity Press, 2010) 210

Vance Havner, a North Carolina pastor who greatly influenced evangelist Billy Graham, preached about the importance of rest in the life of the Christian. Afterward, an irate grumbler came up and scowled at him, saying, "Well, you know who never sleeps? The devil never takes a vacation!" Surrounded by other folks who had listened to his sermon, Havner calmly responded, "Since when am I supposed to be like the devil?"

Next, learn to make lists. We suffer from lack of concentration due to our insistence of constantly accessing the internet and social media. We somehow feel like we need to understand virology, epidemiology, money markets, political science, and everything in between. This flood of useless information interferes with our ability to focus on what is really important in our lives. We must be able to decipher the most important areas of our life and even random information that distracts us.

Start with writing the minor things you have floating in your subconscious; fill up the car, pick up milk, etc. This will free you up for more important things. I use lists to live my daily life and I attempt to keep a small notepad by my bed so that each night I can write down the distractions.

On this day of Sabbath it is important to make an "I want to..." list, but rather than making it about travel or simple selfishness, make it about eternal things. Make it about the on-ramps you have discovered in this book. And under each point, start developing a short plan to implement each one.

Finally, take time to listen, behold, and pray. Make an effort to enter into true worship. Worship as Jesus instructed, "in spirit and in truth."[247] (Upon unwinding and recharging, you will begin to see circumstances differently. The rose-colored eyeglasses of your high-strung existence will fall off and reality will become clear once again. It will allow you to approach God with openness and honesty.

"Worship is giving God the best that he has given you. Be careful what you do with the best you have. Whenever you get a blessing from God, give it back to him as a love gift. Take time to meditate before God and offer the blessing back to him in a deliberate act of worship."[248] Those who enter into worship will find what C. S. Lewis discovered when he realized, "it is in the process of being worshipped that God communicates his presence to men."[249]

Sabbath is an explicitly stated on-ramp that Jesus left us and it will lead us to the healing we need, but more than that it will allow us to move ever closer to wholeness. Bible scholar Frederick Buechner encourages us to, "Take care of yourself so that you can take care of them. A bleeding heart

---

[247] John 4:23,24

[248] Oswald Chambers, *The Complete Works of Oswald Chambers,* (Discovery House Publishers, 2000), 11.

[249] Clive Staples Lewis, *Reflections on the Psalms,* (Harcourt Brace, UK, 1958), 93 .

is of no help to anyone if it bleeds to death."[250] Sabbath moves us beyond self-centeredness and into the arena of true self-care, but only when given the honor and sacredness that God has always intended it to have in our lives. We get this true life, true health, and true wholeness from Sabbath.

The apostle John offered this benediction in his third letter: "Beloved, I pray that you may prosper in all things and be in health, just as your soul prospers." We can see that this place of wholeness — spiritual, emotional, and physical — is a real destination for those living the exponential life. Arriving at this place will allow us to fully engage in all the other on-ramps more deeply. In this place of healed wholeness, we become more effective in our ability to respond to the weaknesses of others. "Whole people see and create wholeness wherever they go; split people see and create splits in everything and everybody."[251] Our healing and our wholeness will extend to the brokenness of those around us.

---

[250] Frederick Buencher, *Listening to Your Life: Daily Meditations with Frederick Buenchner*, (HarperOne, 1992), 340.

[251] Richard Rohr, *Falling Upward: Spirituality for Two Halves of Life*, (Wiley, UK, 2011), 151.

Make it personal

1. Have you ever had a time when leisure got in the way of rest?

2. Examine the Ten Commandments. Do you respect them as a guide for your life?

3. Make a personal to-do list of errands and chores. If you began to complete them one by one, how long would it take you to complete them? What would happen if they didn't get finished?

4. When you have time off, how do you spend it?

Paradoxical Imperatives for Relating to (Citizenship in) Heaven and Earth

10. On-Ramp of Generosity

DISCIPLES OF CHRIST must learn to embrace self-denial. It is a basic Christian value explicit in Jesus' teaching. It is a nonnegotiable for being his disciple. However, we must also grasp for the "yes" when the needs of others are evident without loosening our grip on the "no." This is another paradoxical imperative in the same vein as listening and asking, as wilderness and community. This tension creates space, the space that allows even more of the grace of God to fill our lives. It is a part of the process of becoming exponentially alive.

This "yes" is in response to the on-ramp of radical generosity and starts by simply following Jesus' examples found in the Incarnation. John 1:14 declares, "And the Word became flesh and dwelt among us, and we beheld His glory, the glory as of the only begotten of the Father, full of grace and truth." This beautiful verse reminds us that not only did Jesus come to save the world, but he came in human form to walk some hard miles in our reality. He came to suffer, to struggle, to lose, to cry, to celebrate, to work, to laugh, and to fully live human life. In Matthew chapter 1 we see this reality revealed in another name for Jesus: Emmanuel or "God with us."[252] Hebrews 4:15 reminds us

[252] Matthew 1:23

that "we do not have a High Priest who cannot sympathize with our weaknesses, but was in all points tempted as we are, yet without sin." This is the ultimate definition of condescension; a word that has come to carry a negative connotation, yet at its heart there is much more. He stooped to our level. He chose to feel our pain, our anxiety, and our weight.

American theologian William Willimon clearly explained the necessity of this choice:

> Despite our earnest efforts, we couldn't climb all the way up to God. So what did God do? In an amazing act of condescension, on Good Friday, God climbed down to us, became one with us The story of divine condescension begins on Christmas and ends on Good Friday. We thought, if there is to be business between us and God, we must somehow get up to God. Then God came down, down to the level of the cross, all the way down to the depths of hell. He who knew not sin took on our sin so that we might be free of it. God still stoops, in your life and mine, condescends. "Are you able to drink the cup that I am to drink?" he asked his disciples, before his way up Golgotha. Our answer is an obvious, "No!" His cup is not only the cup of crucifixion and death, it is the bloody, bloody cup that one must drink if one is going to get mixed up in us. Any God who would wander into the human condition, any God who has this thirst to

> pursue us, had better not be too put off by pain, for that's the way we tend to treat our saviors. Any God who tries to love us had better be ready to die for it.[253]

We must see the Incarnation for what it is, the greatest act of radical generosity in the history of humanity.

In this exact place we find the headwaters of radical generosity. When we choose, like Jesus, to get on the same level as someone in need, when we step out of our isolated lives in an attempt to feel their pain, when we attempt to hear the true cause of their anxiety, when we lower our physical and emotional shoulders in an effort to lift the heavy burden that is crushing their life and sucking out their last ounce of hope, even when we may think they do not deserve it — in that moment we are most like Jesus. It is not when we are preaching about him, singing for him, or dancing because of what he has done. It is not when we are speaking in tongues or praying to him, but simply being radically generous to those in need, regardless of their merit.

[253] William Willimon, *Thank God It's Friday: Encountering the Seven Last Words from the Cross*, (Abingdon Press, 2006), 71.

Stop trying to get around it

THE IMPORTANCE of radical generosity in the life of a true disciple is not an option, but an imperative. In the Sermon on the Mount, we see that wonderful word *when* as an entry to Jesus teaching on giving. Not *if* or *possibly* or *when you feel led,* but rather "*when* you give."[254] It indicates a direct order. Look at the parable of the rich man and Lazarus in Luke 16 where Jesus reinforced this imperative:

> There was a certain rich man who was clothed in purple and fine linen and fared sumptuously every day. But there was a certain beggar named Lazarus, full of sores, who was laid at his gate, desiring to be fed with the crumbs which fell from the rich man's table. Moreover the dogs came and licked his sores. So it was that the beggar died, and was carried by the angels to Abraham's bosom. The rich man also died and was buried. And being in torments in Hades, he lifted up his eyes and saw Abraham afar off, and Lazarus in his bosom.[255]

Here we find Lazarus and the unnamed rich man. Unlike many of Christ's parables, this story needed little to no elaboration for its listeners of the day.

---

[254] Matthew 6:2
[255] Luke 16:19-23, KJV

For us, however, there is a bit of fog surrounding the account that needs to be clarified. It states that Lazarus was fed the "crumbs" that fell from the table. In the days of Jesus, when a wealthy family ate, they had loaves of inexpensive bread prepared for the table. The bread served as both utensil and napkin. This predates the personal fork or spoon and made more sense than using valuable hand-woven textile material to wipe off your hands and face. The bread, when broken off, could be used to grab hot food or to scoop up liquids before being discarded from the table. After the meal, servants gathered up the disposable bread and gave it to the beggars and dogs who waited each day at the gates (Matthew 15:27). Then a winner-take-all wrestling match ensued. In the biblical parable, Lazarus and the unidentified rich man die — maybe from a plague or sickness — and go in two separate directions; Lazarus to his reward and the rich man to his punishment.

Something always bothered me about this lesson. A survey of Jesus' preaching reveals he rarely condemned someone to eternal punishment during his preaching, especially during one of his many illustrations. So why did this man fall under judgment? What was his sin? We know that being rich in and of itself is not a sin. We are not told that this rich man did something immoral in his acquisition of wealth. We are not told that he cheated or stole his vast riches. He wore nice clothes and had expensive tastes. These may not be in step with Jesus' teaching, but they wouldn't have landed the man in condemnation. We know that he gave Lazarus his scrap bread each day. To us, the meaning is obscure. To Jesus' listeners, it would have been understood.

In Jesus' time, a common Jewish nursery rhyme asserted, "Don't do to others what you do not want them to do to you." It doesn't sound catchy or roll off your tongue, but it does sound familiar. It makes sense that when Jesus laid out his Golden Rule he appropriated a cultural idiom that had negative qualities and flipped it into something completely positive. The Jews taught their kids that they should not kill or steal. And in one fell swoop, Jesus changed it. He told them to stop "not doing" and start "doing." In Matthew 7:12[256] he said, "In everything, do unto others, as you would have them to do unto you, for this sums up the Law and Prophets."

Solomon laid down an imperative in the third chapter of Proverbs, commanding that people of faith should not withhold good from those to whom it is due, when it is in the power of your hand to do so. Do not say to your neighbor, 'Go, and come back, And tomorrow I will give it,' when you have it with you."[257] Thus it wasn't that the rich man did something wrong. It was that he had not done all he could to allay the need at his doorstep each day. He likely justified himself by saying, "That guy has always been

[256] NIV

[257] Proverbs 3:27-28

a poor beggar and he will always be a poor beggar. He comes from a family of beggars and there is nothing that will change that."

In James 4:17, this reasoning is dismantled: "If anyone, then, knows the good they ought to do and doesn't do it, it is sin for them."[258] The sin is indifference, in not doing something we know to be right when it is in our power to do it. If we do nothing, we allow ourselves to fall into the sin of thinking that nothing will change, the sin of allowing ourselves to justify our hardheartedness, or the sin of not "getting on their level" as Jesus did for us. This was the rich man's sin, which put him where none of us ever wants to be.

This on-ramp is a supernatural act with unbelievable potential. When we extend it, we are at our most Christ-like. It is one of the few things we can do to share the grace we have received, the unmerited favor that we have freely been given by God. The decision to be radically generous — regardless of how much we think the person we are extending it to may deserve it — places us in the tradition of God who sent his Son to save us "while we were yet sinners."[259]

This does not mean that we take on the role of Jesus and somehow become their saviors. The grace we share will either be received or rejected. It may open the door so

---

258 NIV

259 Romans 5:8, KJV

that the soul receiving it can be saved when the unending and limitless grace that comes straight from the fountain of God's perfect love rushes in. It may not instantly open up eternity to the person receiving it, but it could extend their life long enough for their eternity to be impacted.

Misplaced treasure will get you in trouble

THIS CONVERSATION about radical generosity lands us in the center of the action. We are prohibited from withholding good when we have the option to share it. This revelation might make us a bit uncomfortable, maybe even causing a bit of good old-fashioned Holy Spirit conviction. When we examine our life and realize we have failed in the area of generosity — one that is so clear in the Old and New Testaments — it should have an intense effect on us.

We squirm and slide in our comfortable chairs, in our gated community thinking of all the needs we drive past each day that have just become part of the landscape. We say to ourselves that they will never change. We do nothing ostensibly wrong, but we do nothing overtly right. We begin to search for a way to just make the feeling go away. We phone our pastor or consult the Bible looking for a specific number or an exact percentage of our income to make this feeling go away. The problem is Jesus never gave us one.

Generosity is a condition of the heart. Jesus' confrontation with the rich young ruler in Mark 10:17-22 was one of compassion. It says, "Then Jesus, looking at him, loved him, and said to him, 'One thing you lack: Go your way, sell whatever you have and give to the poor, and you will have treasure in heaven; and come, take up the cross, and follow Me.' But he was sad at this word, and went away sorrowful, for he had great possessions."

In this instance we see that Jesus commanded him to sell it all. Then we read something puzzling in Matthew 27:57, "Now when evening had come, there came a rich man from Arimathea, named Joseph, who himself had also become a disciple of Jesus." So Joseph of Arimathea was a disciple and wealthy, yet we never hear of Jesus exhorting him to sell it all. Why the discrepancy? To answer that, we need to understand what Jesus taught about what we call treasure.

Returning to the Sermon on the Mount, we find that Jesus places a power on treasure that he does not place on anything else. He describes it as something with the power to move our heart, a power not afforded to prayer, fasting, worship, or any other religious exercise. Smack in the middle of Jesus' longest sermon, he dropped a truth bomb:

> Do not lay up for yourselves treasures on earth, where moth and rust destroy and where thieves break in and steal; but lay up for yourselves treasures in heaven,

> where neither moth nor rust destroys and where thieves do not break in and steal. For where your treasure is, there your heart will be also.[260]

The first two verses are great reminders for us to be careful in our accumulation of stuff while on earth, but the greatest revelation is found in the last line. Many think their treasure follows their heart, but that is not true. Your heart follows your treasure. It has the power to move your entire being.

You would be hard pressed to find something else in Scripture afforded that much leverage. Your treasure has the power to transform you. If it has the power to move your heart toward God, it must conversely possess the power to move you away from him. This realization alone will not shield us from this reality.

"The heart clings to collected treasure. Stored-up possessions get between me and God. Where my treasure is, there my trust, my security, my comfort, my God. Treasure means idolatry."[261] For that reason, it is easy to believe the tradition that alleges Martin Luther was keen on preaching three conversions: the conversion of the head, the heart, and the pocketbook. He knew full well that when God has your treasure, he has all of you.

---

[260] Matthew 6:19-21, ESV

[261] Dietrich Bonhoeffer, *Discipleship*, (Fortress Press, UK, 2015), 134.

So when we are looking for the answer to the question posed by the rich young ruler, Joseph of Arimathea, and Jesus, it is one of misplaced treasure. We must realize that everything we have — all of our treasure — will serve as either an implement or an obstacle to our relationship with God. If my treasure is in the right place, much like a giant pry bar with unlimited leverage, it will draw me to God. If it is in the wrong place, it will be a stumbling block, even if I am doing everything else right in my pursuit of God.

Some still want to know how to know when they have given enough. In *Mere Christianity,* C. S. Lewis answered that question best:

> I do not believe one can settle how much we ought to give. I am afraid the only safe rule is to give more than we can spare. In other words, if our expenditure on comforts, luxuries, amusements, etc. is up to the standard common among those with the same income as our own, we are probably giving away too little. If our charities do not at all pinch or hamper us, I should say they are too small. There ought to be things we should like to do and cannot do because our charitable expenditure excludes them.[262]

[262] C.S. Lewis, *Mere Christianity*, (Touchstone, 1996), 82.

When I have practiced radical generosity, it caused me to sacrifice my wants. It pinched and hampered my self-centeredness. That level of generosity has ensured me that my treasure was where it was supposed to be. Anytime I have allowed myself to step into radical generosity, I have walked away richer than when I started. Only through experience can we understand what Jesus meant in Acts 20:35: "It is more blessed to give than to receive."

You are richer than you think

AS MANY OF US KNOW from our scars, experience is the best teacher. This is true of the pain of failure and the thrill of obedience. When we consider the on-ramp of radical generosity, the most common error is limiting the application of generosity to assets and incomes. If you have money, you give it; if you don't, then put an asterisk beside your name to be exonerated on the final exam, such thinking goes. However, the generosity Jesus taught his disciples was too radical to be limited to a merely fiscal act.

This is not to say it was some esoteric exercise limited to cave dwellers. Jesus gave us practical instruction specific to money. For instance, Luke 21:1-4 reports:

> And He looked up and saw the rich putting their gifts into the treasury, and He saw also a certain poor widow

> putting in two mites. So He said, "Truly I say to you that this poor widow has put in more than all; for all these out of their abundance have put in offerings for God, but she out of her poverty put in all the livelihood that she had.

God doesn't view magnanimity the same way humans do. George Mueller noted, "We are accepted and judged by God on the basis of what is in our possession and what we do with it rather than what we don't have."[263] There is an equalizing reality found in Jesus' teaching. He is not measuring us according to what we give, but according to how much we have left over.

That reality extends his command for radical generosity in the areas of mercy and forgiveness:

> Therefore be merciful, just as your Father also is merciful. Judge not, and you shall not be judged. Condemn not, and you shall not be condemned. Forgive, and you will be forgiven. Give, and it will be given to you: good measure, pressed down, shaken together, and running over will be put into your bosom. For with the same measure that you use, it will be measured back to you.[264]

---

[263] George Mueller, *The Autobiography of George Mueller*, (First Love Publications), 40.

[264] Luke 6:36-38

Here we find Jesus' prosperity gospel, but not in the way it has mutated in some preachers' eyes. The promise here is for prosperity to those who are generous in mercy and forgiveness. Those qualities when given will be returned to the giver. Radical generosity always offers a reward for those who practice it and a bitter pill for those who don't. "One gives freely, yet grows all the richer; another withholds what he should give, and only suffers want."[265]

This same imperative is at play when Jesus commands his first followers to spend and be spent in their effort to share the good news they received, the insight they encountered, and the eternal truth they grasped as a result of accepting Jesus' invitation to take on his yoke. He told them to become radically generous by sharing their personal experiences with others.

In Acts 1:8, he told them to become his "witnesses... in Jerusalem, and in all Judea and Samaria, and to the end of the earth."[266] After his resurrection, he wanted them to collectively invest their resources, as well as their time and effort, to turn the world upside down by making true disciples. He told them, "Go therefore and make disciples of all the nations, baptizing them in the name of the Father and of the Son and of the Holy Spirit, teaching them to observe all things that I have commanded you."[267]

---

265 Proverbs 11:24, ESV
266 ESV
267 Matthew 28:19-20a, NIV

This is not merely an invitation to participate in the church as consumers. These are not on-ramps reserved for pastors or preachers. They are for anyone who is truly his disciple, especially those striving to live the exponential life. Let those imperatives seep into your subconscious and ask yourself about your level of generosity in the areas of witness, making disciples, and teaching what Jesus taught.

Radical generosity — whether with money, time, talents, experiences, mercy, forgiveness, or anything else — always points us outward to others also created in the image of God. As true worshippers of God, we know we don't have to be rich to be generous. In a life of artificial intelligence, social media, and an increasingly virtual existence, it allows us to remember that we are all still in the same boat. It makes us focus on the needs of others so that we can forget about ourselves for a moment of our self-absorbed existence. We remember it is a blessing to give, especially to "the least of these."[268] In loving those in need, we are loving Jesus himself. We can learn from Robert Louis Stevenson's observation of the Polynesian culture's generous traditions; you can always give without loving, but you can never love without giving.[269] Let us look not only at our wallets, but also into our hearts so we can give more than we are comfortable giving each day of our life.

---

[268] Matthew 25:31-46

[269] Robert Louis Stevenson, *Robert Louis Stevenson: In the South Seas.* A Foot-note in History, (Scribner, 1896), 84-85.

One pitfall we must avoid is to seek out minimums for measuring our giving. Some think that as long as they tithe to their local church, they are OK. That is simply not true. As we saw earlier, radical generosity extends beyond our wallet and finances. It flows into our heart, our thoughts, and even our words. How then do we practically practice radical generosity in our daily lives? Maybe the best understanding is given by Og Mandino in the fifth scroll in his book *The Greatest Salesman in the World* when he encouraged his reader to make a choice. "Beginning today," he wrote, "treat everyone you meet as if they were going to be dead by midnight. Extend to them all the care, kindness and understanding you can muster, and do it with no thought of any reward. Your life will never be the same again."[270] That is radical generosity in its simplest form, and as Christians who desire to become fruitful, it must be lived out every day, not just on the days when the offering plate is passed.

There is a reason I prefaced this imperative with the word *radical*. It is crazy to think that anyone in their right mind would be generous in our self-centered, self-serving world. It is a rare occurrence with those we are supposed to love and live in community with, and practically as common as a UFO sighting when extended to our enemies. In an ever-increasing atmosphere of selfishness, even the simplest acts of generosity become radical.

---

[270] Og Mandino, *A Better Way to Live*, (Random House Publishers, UK, 2010), 90.

When Jesus commanded his followers to be generous with their time, belongings, talents, mercy, forgiveness, and prayers, he made his expectations explicit. It went beyond self-love, past family ties, outside of church affiliation, and directly toward those we least want to bless: our enemies. Those who persecute and despise us and those who say things behind our backs and to our faces simply because we are disciples of Christ are to be the recipients of our generosity. What if we think they don't deserve it? What if we think the act will be wasted? Do it anyway. That is not for us to debate. Maybe he set this high bar that extends to everyone to include even our enemies because they need a little extra dose of grace. Perhaps the limited, secondhand grace we freely give will open the door for God's limitless grace to come flooding into their lives.

This on-ramp of radical generosity leads us to a place of firm footing by leading us to continually live in the position of compassion. Frederick Buechner said, "Compassion is sometimes the fatal capacity for feeling what it is like to live inside somebody else's skin. It is the knowledge that there can never really be any peace and joy for me until there is peace and joy finally for you too."[271] This place of compassion is exponential. It is the place Paul pushed toward when he admonished the church in Philippians 2:1-11:

---

[271] Frederic Brussar and Mary Ann Brussat, *Spiritual Literacy: Reading the Sacred in Everyday Life,* (Scribner, 1998), 91.

> Therefore if there is any consolation in Christ, if any comfort of love, if any fellowship of the Spirit, if any affection and mercy, fulfill my joy by being like-minded, having the same love, being of one accord, of one mind. Let nothing be done through selfish ambition or conceit, but in lowliness of mind let each esteem others better than himself. Let each of you look out not only for his own interests, but also for the interests of others.

This compassion that comes as a result of radical generosity has led Christians over the ages to preach the gospel in every language and to plant churches around the world, but it has also been the cause for them to establish public schools, public hospitals, abolish slavery, establish democratic governments, and define the modern concept of human rights. I agree with 19th century preacher Henry Ward Beecher who said, "Compassion will cure more sins than condemnation."[272] When you open yourself to generosity you are standing on the bedrock of compassion. You can change the world.

---

[272] Henry Ward Beecher, *Life Thoughts*, (1858), 158.

Make it personal

1. How much do you need to feel at peace financially? Is it the same answer you would have given in the past?

2. How do you respond when you are asked to give?

3. Are there things you know you should be giving to others, such as grace, forgiveness, and mercy that you aren't making available?

4. Besides monetary resources, what can you offer to those in need?

11. On-Ramp of Beholding

BEFORE I MADE the effort to better understand the term, when I heard the word *behold*, I could not help but drift to an often-satirized scene from many B movies from the Saturday morning television marathons of my childhood, like the fearless explorer who stumbled onto a Stone Age tribe bent on eating him, or at least killing him. After a predictable series of events, the explorer would be found either on the edge of an endless cliff or a lava-filled volcano. Standing at death's door, he would pull out his trusty windproof lighter, which he would light and proclaim "Behold!" The natives would bow down to the display of power provided by the small piece of tin and impeccable timing of the explorer. Likewise I recalled the magician who cut his assistant in half. Upon completion, he separated the two "sides" of his assistant and proclaimed "Behold!" All campy television programs aside, I cannot truly hope to step into the full exponential life without beholding.

Behold is a word that has fallen out of use in our modern world, except in satire and magic. The Bible, on the other hand, takes beholding very seriously. Its use has faded from many modern translations that opt for words such as *look, listen,* or *see.* The translators of the English Standard Version, however, concluded that these do not convey the word's true meaning. They give a heartfelt justification for retaining it in the opening notes of their work:

> Although 'Look!' and 'See!' and 'Listen!' would be workable in some contexts, in many others these words lack sufficient weight and dignity. Given the principles of 'essentially literal' translation, it is important not to leave "hinneh" and "idou" completely untranslated, and so to lose the intended emphasis in the original languages. The older and more formal word 'behold' has usually been retained, therefore, as the best available option for conveying the original sense of meaning.[273]

In the King James Version, the word is used over 1,200 times! Even though *behold* may fall somewhat strangely on our modern ears, scholars point to the importance of researching it, familiarizing ourselves with it, and with an eye on keeping it in our vernacular.

So what does it mean to behold if not simply looking, listening, or seeing? Researcher Leah Zuidema writes,

> Perhaps we've lost something with the disappearance of the word behold from our Scripture translations and its corresponding erasure from our culture. Do we really know how to behold? How to stop still, to cease all else,

[273] English Standard Version, Study Bible, (Crossway Publishers, 2008), translator's note.

> to give our full attention and searching gaze to what is before us? In our multi-tasking, fast-paced world, we are in the habit of looking everywhere at once–with the result that nothing (and no one) truly has our deep and undivided attention. We are so captivated...by new ideas, activities, and social connections that we forget to stop and behold.[274]

The details of this imperative are best understood by illustrating it in action.

When I asked a friend what he thought it meant to behold, his answer did not surprise me. He had just become a father for the first time and said it simply means "To take a long and loving look at something. Like a father or a mother looks over their newborn baby." It is noticing the features, even the most subtle; the freckles, the shape of the ears, the lips, the fingers. It is deeply concentrating in an effort to see the contours and to capture the essence. The sense of beholding overtook me when I held each of my children at birth. I felt it the first time I saw the Grand Canyon. I looked for what seemed like endless hours into the shadows, the cracks, the crevices, searching diligently for the contours.

---

[274] DeHaan, C., & Bair, J. (2021, Aug. 18). "*Lent: Behold! behold! behold!*" *-inallthings*.org in All things. Exploring the implications of Christ's presence in all of life. Retrieved from https://inallthings.org/lent-behold-behold-behold.

I again experienced it when I visited Holland and stood before Rembrandt's *Night Watch*. I searched the immense work of art for every final detail I could find. I did not rush. I lost track of time in my searching, all in an effort to find the contours. It happens each time I listen to an amazing piece of music by a composer like Mozart, Bach, or the more modern Arvo Pärt. I lean in and attempt to find the contours in the music. This occurs in a spiritual sense as well. It is pausing and leaning in with all available senses as I am being drawn deeper in awe of God's greatness. It is taking the time to look for God's fingerprints. Like a small child roving through a house while snacking on a chocolate bar will leave a trail, God's prints are everywhere. But like those on a window or mirror, they are only seen with effort. That effort is beholding. It is also simply lingering and holding onto a "God moment" a bit longer and allowing it to draw you deeper into understanding, deeper than you have been before. Like deep sea divers who need the help of lead weights to pull them deeper into the unknown, we too, can take on the task of beholding and allow it to pull us further up and further in.

Unlike when we behold something in the nonspiritual sense, and are simply left speechless or a moment takes our breath away, this paradoxical imperative that Jesus commands has an even greater impact on our lives. When we behold, we are holding something long enough in our working memory so that it will find its place in our long-term memory. If we do not take the time this on-ramp requires, then we fall into what James warned us of doing when he wrote, "For if anyone is a hearer of the word and not a doer, he is like a man observing his natural face in a mirror; for he observes himself, goes away, and immediately forgets what kind of man he was."[275]

When we truly behold God, our trust grows, as if we are putting more and more of our weight down in our relationship with our Heavenly Father. Beholding God will eventually lead us to the realization that we are indeed not just floating specks of cosmic matter blown around by circumstantial winds. But we realize we ourselves are in fact being held by our loving Creator. As Early Church father Irenaeus said, "The glory of God is man fully alive and the glory of man is the beholding of God."[276]

We behold him by what is revealed in his Word

ONE OF THE FIRST PLACES we must choose to pause is in the Bible, but not for just a casual visit. If we want to behold God in the Bible, we need to be ready to

---

[275] James 1:23-24

[276] Irenaeus. *Against Heresies*, Book IV, Chapter 20, (Create Space, 2012), 419.

growl. Several years ago, when reading *Eat This Book* by Eugene Peterson, I found in the opening pages a lesson that has altered my approach to the Word of God. Peterson focuses on the importance of our posture as we engage the eternal Word of God. The title is taken from Revelation 10:9-10 when the seer is given a sacred scroll and mysteriously ordered to eat it. He then takes a look at Isaiah's vision of a lion growling over his prey.[277]

He notes that the Hebrew verb is to be understood as *growling*, yet most modern translations of this text usually use *meditates* or *watch over*. He encourages us to approach the Bible as a lion over its prey or a dog growling over a bone. I have taken the growling challenge as an exercise in beholding the Scripture. Before I read quickly. Now I read and I am ready to write it down. I carry it with me (usually as a note stuck under the clear cover of my cellphone). I purposefully dig it back up. I revisit the words. And, like a dog, I hold onto and chew on what God has said to me and what I have beheld in an attempt to get the very last drop of marrow out of it. Beholding is holding what you have read and looking longer. The Scriptures are to be enjoyed, beheld, and growled over.

One way of doing this is by choosing to sit down when we come across one of the places that God proclaimed "behold" and leaning in and attempting to see the contours of

[277] Isaiah 31:4

what God is saying. When we do this we create a "thin place" in our soul. Another way is to focus on the depths of what has been revealed to us about God. I call this the infinite attributes of God. These include the Trinity (One in Three, Three in One), omniscience (all-knowing), omnipresence (everywhere present), eternal (no beginning or end), and unconditional and unmerited love (cannot be earned, only acknowledged and received). They are the limitless characteristics of God that are a challenge for our finite minds to comprehend or contain.

As Paul taught the church at Corinth, "We fix our eyes not on what is seen, but on what is unseen. For what is seen is temporary, but what is unseen is eternal."[278] The infinite attributes of God are not the seen, but the unseen parts of God. John Cassian saw our time of focused thinking as "the one thing needful is a mind which, regardless of all else, is fixed on God alone, and rejoices in the contemplation of His perfection."[279] I have come to see it as this type of deep pool that we can dive into, although we will never touch the bottom. As John Calvin explained, "Man with all his shrewdness is as stupid about understanding by himself the mysteries of God, as an ass is incapable of understanding

---

[278] 2 Corinthians 4:18, NIV

[279] Cornelius Cornelii a Lapide, *The Great Commentary of Cornelius À Lapide*, Volume 4,(John Hodges), 266.

musical harmony."[280] But this inability should never keep us from jumping into the deep end of the pool. Instead, it should serve as a certainty that we can go further up and further in without fear of running out of space.

There is a second group I call the visible attributes of God or the Incarnation. These are the truths revealed through the life of Jesus Christ. They include his virgin birth, his life, death, resurrection, and ascension, as well as his teachings to his disciples. These all serve as windows into the Trinity. They serve to illuminate our understanding of God. Puritan John Owen wrote:

> Make up your mind that to behold the glory of God by beholding the glory of Christ is the greatest privilege which is given to believers in this life. This is the dawning of heaven. It is the first taste of that heavenly glory which God has prepared for us, for this is eternal life, to know the Father and Jesus Christ whom he has sent.[281]

This mind-boggling and life-changing event of beholding "the glory of Christ" does not happen by chance, no more than a child can draw a perfect replica of the *Mona Lisa* with their box of eight crayons with just one glance. It takes time, effort, and faith.

---

[280] Steve Wilkens, *Faith and Reason: Three Views*, (Intervarsity Press, 2014), 25.

[281] John Owen, *The Glory of Christ*, (Banner of Truth, 1965), 22-23.

As Martin Luther stated in his *Large Catechism*, "We could never come to recognize the Father's favor and grace were it not for the Lord Christ, who is a mirror of the Father's heart."[282] We take time to peer through those windows in an attempt to catch a clear glimpse of the true nature of God, specifically his infinite attributes. We see the challenges laid before us twice in the Book of Hebrews in 3:1 and 12:2, where we are reminded to "fix your thoughts on Jesus" and to "fix our eyes on Jesus."[283] The Incarnation is of such importance, yet so underused in our modern church as we are reminded from Luther's words to the troubled Barbara Lisskirchen when he encouraged her in a time of weakness:

> The highest of all God's commands is this, that we hold up before our eyes the image of his dear son, our Lord Jesus Christ. Every day he should be the excellent mirror wherein we behold how much God loves us and how well, in his infinite goodness, he has cared for us in that he gave his dear Son for us. Contemplate Christ given for us. Then, God willing, you will feel better.[284]

---

[282] Martin Luther, *The Book of Concord: The Confessions of the Evangelical Lutheran Church*, ed. Theodore Gerhardt Tappert,(Fortress Press, 1959), 419.

[283] NIV

[284] Martin Luther, *Letters of Spiritual Counsel*, (Regent College Publishing, 2003), 117.

It is important to remember that our desire is to know God so that we can love him even more, redefine our understanding of truth, and reach the place where our ideas are shaped by the truth of God instead of the shifting sands of our feelings. We must strive to align ourselves in truth as Jonathan Edwards did so we reach the understanding that, "Truth, in the general, may be defined, after the most strict and metaphysical manner. The consistency and agreement of our ideas with the ideas of God."[285]

I encourage you not to fall into the trap that has commonly overtaken many in our modern church. It concerns one of the central elements of the Incarnation, perhaps the very one that makes us most uncomfortable. We warmly behold the nativity of Jesus with its warm colors, as well the scenes of the victorious resurrection, yet we trip over the cross of Christ and his sufferings. Even more so than in the day of Paul, when he wrote in 1 Corinthians 1:18-25 that the Cross seems like "foolishness" to those outside of the church, yet to those of us who are pursuing the exponential life promised by Jesus, we realize that "it is the power of God." To some, Paul says it will serve as a "stumbling block" and to others nothing more than "silliness."

Yet beholding the cross of Jesus is what pulled two of the Lord's disciples, Joseph of Arimathea and Nicodemus, out of hiding: Both had much more to lose than the rabble

---

[285]Henry Rogers, *The Works of Jonathan Edwards, A.M.: With an Essay on His Genius and Writings. Volume 1,* (W. Ball, UK, 1839) cclxvii.

Jesus had selected as his core team. In John 19, we see them emerge from the shadows and take their place beside him when everyone else has fled the scene. When we behold the Cross, like Joseph and Nicodemus, we are changed and filled with courage to step out and be counted. Paul again helps us to understand that the Cross is part of the plan, even when we struggle to wrap our heads around it. In 1 Corinthians 1:25, he writes, "Because the foolishness of God is wiser than men; and the weakness of God is stronger than men."

We can also take time to chew on the metaphors throughout Scripture. It is important for us to realize the limited power of literal language when attempting to understand the unknowable God. A number of examples of metaphors are found in the Book of John. Jesus refers to himself as the "Good Shepherd," "The Door," "The Light of the World," and "The Vine." It's best to take a moment to mind our metaphors to ensure that we are not reducing the grandeur of the unknowable, holy Creator of the universe into a single definition. Chris Hall taught me that, "a metaphor is meant to bear the weight of glory, but if we put too much on it, it will snap."[286]

Still, each one gives us insight and when we behold them we learn to hold more than one at a time. Learning to hold more than one metaphor will allow us to know God more

---

[286] Chris Hall, from a talk given at Renovaré Institute.

deeply. How can we be content to know only one facet of a God of infinite facets? Most only reach Savior or Lord, yet God offers Healer, Teacher, Lover, and Friend to us as well. Accumulating metaphors allows us to have a firmer grasp on who we already know God to be, without loosening our grip on what we already have in hand. All metaphors are incomplete simply because God is incomprehensible. You do not possess enough intellect to wrap around him. But that should not prevent you from striving to know him more fully.

Our beholding will become habitual. Our minds drift where we have conditioned them to drift. They go into the ruts that have been worn in our subconscious as a result of our most concentrated and focused thinking. Thus, beholding should be practiced until it becomes the pathway our mind drifts into when allowed to wander. We must engage in the process, too, if we hope to overcome the bad thinking habits that run our daily life.

Most of us confess to be Christians, yet too many of us must admit that God is not the focus of our daily deep thinking. Other images and ideas are impulsively moving us along. Some are sinful while others are nothing more than distractions. When we choose to behold, what we are actually doing is simply putting God firmly into the driver's seat. We behold him when we choose to savor and to hold on a little longer to what he is saying.

We behold him in his Creation

IT IS IMPORTANT to observe creation. As the apostle Paul noted in Romans 1:20, "For since the creation of the world God's invisible qualities — his eternal power and divine nature — have been clearly seen, being understood from what has been made, so that people are without excuse."[287]

Creation is, in God's terms, the first gospel written for all to observe. I love to find time to focus my concentration on the whole work of my Creator. As naturalist John Muir wrote, "All wilderness seems to be full of tricks and plans to drive and draw us up into God's light."[288] The small insects and the larger-than-reality vistas will lead us into greater understanding, as they did for George Washington Carver. He confessed, "I love to think of nature as an unlimited broadcasting station, through which God speaks to us every hour, if we will only tune in."[289]

The Italian mystic Paul of the Cross encouraged us in this way:

---

[287] NIV

[288] John Muir, *Nature Writings: The Story of My Boyhood and Youth, My First Summer in the Sierra, the Mountains of California,* (Library of America, 1997), 298.

[289] George Washington Carver Scott G. Cady and Christopher L. Webber, *A Year with American Saints,* (Church Publishing, 2006), 319.

> Listen to the sermon preached to you by the flowers, the trees, the shrubs, the sky, and the whole world. Notice how they preach to you a sermon full of love, of praise of God, and how they invite you to glorify the sublimity of that sovereign Artist who has given them being.[290]

When we behold the Lord in nature, we realize that "God dwells in His creation and is everywhere indivisibly present in all His works. He is transcendent above all His works even while He is immanent within them."[291] To some, this is a bit "out there" and smells like something other than your grandmother's Christianity.

But this is not some exercise in New Age philosophy, as Sandu Sundar Singh defends: "The Indian Seer lost God in Nature; the Christian mystic, on the other hand, finds God in Nature. The Hindu mystic believes that God and Nature are one and the same; the Christian mystic knows that there must be a Creator to account for the universe."[292] In the wilderness, I have observed some of the greatest sermons ever preached: in the desert sunrise, in the rippling waters of a mountain stream, in the blooming mountain rose covered in snow at 10,000 feet, in a carpet of butterflies brought out by the passing rain, in the smile of my

[290] Tri Robinson, *Saving God's Green Earth*, (Ampelon Publishing, 2006), 133.

[291] A.W. Tozer, *The Pursuit of God*, (Gospel Light, 2013), 62.

[292] Friedrich Heiler, *The Gospel of Sandu Sundar Singh*, (Creative Media Partners, 2018), 143.

child, and in the beauty of the intricacy of my father's hand. When you are beholding God's creation, "It is the details in which lies the beauty."[293]

Once you find the wilderness, it is important to allow your heart and even your body to wander a bit. This wandering isn't into other tasks or what you need to be doing besides being in the wilderness. If possible, lose track of time. Teach yourself to slow down. Start with your breathing, then let it pass to your praying, and all the way to your walking. Stop and look for longer than you normally would. Make an effort to see the contours of God in his creation.

We behold him in the creations of his Creation

THOSE WHO ARE GIFTED with creativity in the arts are deeply in tune with the reality that we are all created in God's image and that he is Creator of everything.[294] We can see that God has tipped his hand throughout Scripture to reveal that he has given certain artists even greater capacities. In Exodus 35:35, we read, "He has filled them with skill to do every sort of work done

---

[293] C. H. Spurgeon from a sermon preached July 22, 1866, at Metropolitan Tabernacle.

[294] Colossians 1:15-16

by an engraver or by a designer or by an embroiderer in blue and purple and scarlet yarns and fine twined linen, or by a weaver by any sort of workman or skilled designer."[295] As they built the tabernacle in the wilderness and then the temple in Jerusalem, it is apparent that God was leveraging art as a form of worship.

"The temple was covered with precious stones for beauty. There was no pragmatic reason for the precious stones. They had no utilitarian purpose. God simply wanted beauty in the temple. God is interested in beauty."[296] Later, in the New Testament, those who work — whether in a field, an office, or an artistic workshop — are commended by the apostle Paul to work "with all your heart, as working for the Lord, not for human masters."[297]

For too long, as evangelical, Spirit-filled disciples, we have not given art its proper place. Our history comes from storefront churches, house churches, metal buildings, or old malls instead of Gothic cathedrals adorned with art. I admire the drive to just "make it happen," but sometimes in our efforts to become completely practical, we lose the ability to behold the beauty of God in art. If we are not careful, we give up a powerful element in the exponential life. As musician Michael Card said, "A hunger for beauty

---

[295] ESV

[296] Francis Schaeffer, *Art and the Bible*, (Kindle Edition, IVP Classics, 1973), 26.

[297] Colossians 3:23-24, NIV

is at its heart a hunger for God."[298] Lamentably, many have lost their hunger for beauty.

Art is viewed with skepticism because it has a mind of its own, and left unredeemed, it will land us in the gutter of carnality. We see this in the world of music, film, and print. Yet it is God who has gifted us with this creativity; whether we use it for his glory depends on us. Let us not throw the baby out with the bathwater simply because it is hard to find good Christian artists. I agree with the astronomer Galileo when he quipped to his religious detractors, "I do not feel obliged to believe that the same God who has endowed us with senses, reason, and intellect has intended us to forgo their use."[299] God has given us the ability to create. Let us create the most beautiful works of art possible, knowing that in doing so we are glorifying God. As Henry Wadsworth Longfellow stated in his poem *Michael Angelo*, we must understand that "art is the gift of God, and must be used unto His glory. That in art is highest which aims at this."[300]

Thomas Merton, whose books on prayer and the spiritual life were bestsellers throughout the last century, found that "Music and art and poetry attune the soul to

---

[298] J. Scott McElroy, *Creative Church Handbook: Releasing the Power of the Arts in Your Congregation*, (Intervarsity Press, 2015), 264.

[299] David Tuohy, *Philosophy, Theology and the Jesuit Tradition: 'The Eye of Love'*, (Bloomsbury Publishing, 2017), 32.

[300] Sykes, *Canterbury Book of Spiritual Quotations*, (Hymns Ancient and Modern, 2007), 18.

God."[301] When we make an effort to see the contours or the fingerprints of God in art, we are allowing it to pull us deeper into the act of worship and consequently open our being to our Creator. Some may feel a reservation that evangelical theologian and writer Francis Schaeffer confessed when he wrote in his book *Art and the Bible*:

> As evangelical Christians, we have tended to relegate art to the very fringe of life. The rest of human life we feel is more important. Despite our constant talk about the lordship of Christ, we have narrowed its scope to a very small area of reality. We have misunderstood the concept of the lordship of Christ over the whole man and the whole of the universe and have not taken to us the riches that the Bible gives us for ourselves, for our lives, and for our culture.[302]

We have limited God, thinking that somehow God is confined to communicating with us through the Bible and nothing else. Yet this constraint reveals a lack of faith as he goes on to proclaim, "If Christianity is really true, then it involves the whole man, including his intellect and creativeness."[303]

---

[301] Thomas Merton, *No Man is an Island*, (Mariner Books, 2002), 36.

[302] Francis Schaeffer, *A Christian View of the Bible as Truth*, (Crossway Books, 1994), 375.

[303] Francis Schaeffer ibid, 376.

The longer you behold, the more you see

BEHOLDING IS STRIVING to just be with God. "This is what you are to do. Lift your heart up to the Lord with a gentle stirring of love, desiring him for his own sake and not for his gifts."[304] It is an effort involving body, soul, mind, and strength; to be in His loving presence; to make him the center of our thoughts; to allow him to respond with us concerning our questions; to listen to his guidance; and ultimately to maintain a constant conversation with him. The result is a constant stretching of our understanding to a greater commitment and a greater love toward God. We begin to see things differently as we understand the depths of God, the Incarnation, true blessedness, creation, and our unanswered questions.

It is like the blind man in Mark chapter 8:22-26 whom Jesus healed in a rather unorthodox way:

> Then He came to Bethsaida; and they brought a blind man to Him, and begged Him to touch him. So He took the blind man by the hand and led him out of the town. And when He had spit on his eyes and put His hands on him, He asked him if he saw anything. And he looked up and said, "I see men like trees, walking."

---

[304] James Finley, *The Awakening Call: Fostering Intimacy with God,* (Ave Maria Press, 1984), 70.

> Then He put His hands on his eyes again and made him look up. And he was restored and saw everyone clearly. Then He sent him away to his house, saying, "Neither go into the town, nor tell anyone in the town."

Many things, in the beginning, were unclear, but rather than simply throwing in the towel, he returned to the source and continued deeper. Eventually getting a clearer view of what was truly going on, early church theologian Jerome explained,

> Christ laid his hands upon his eyes that he might see all things clearly, so through visible things he might understand things invisible which the eye has not seen, that after the film of sin is removed, he might clearly behold the state of his soul with the eye of a clean heart.[305]

Beholding prepares us to look past the simple face value of our situation so that we can truly believe in God. It allows us to possess truth with which we will navigate daily life, rather than falling prey to those emotions in us which scream the loudest. It cultivates a deeper faith and gives us a reason to keep pressing forward in our sometimes lonely process of becoming fruitful. Our long-term goal of the ex-

---

305 Thomas C. Oden, Christopher A. Hall, *Ancient Christian Commentary on Scripture: Mark*, (InterVarsity Press, 2014), 103.

ponential life must be broken down into smaller signposts. I have made progress by keeping a daily goal, as noted by John Ortberg:

> Many Christians expend so much energy and worry trying not to sin. The goal is not to try to sin less. In all your efforts to keep from sinning, what are you focusing on? Sin. God wants you to focus on him. To be with him. "Abide in me." Just relax and learn to enjoy his presence. Every day is a collection of moments, 86,400 seconds in a day. How many of them can you live with God? Start where you are and grow from there. God wants to be with you every moment.[306]

Beholding is a choice. As the old saying goes, "None are as blind, as those who refuse to see." Those who choose not to see or hear what God is doing are called "foolish" in Jeremiah 5:21 because they are not using their full facilities to seek God. Jesus even references this in Matthew 13 when he explained his use of parables instead of old-fashioned "straight talk." He expected his disciples to behold the stories he taught and not just pass them by. When we choose to behold God, we will eventually realize that God is waiting and wants to be with us every moment. He is just a thought or a question away.

---

[306] John Ortberg, *Soul Keeping: Caring for the Most Important Part of You*, (Zondervan, 2014), 139.

The on-ramp of beholding will keep us in a state of awe and wonder as opposed to the fog of existence that most humans dwell in. Albert Einstein understood this when he proclaimed, "He who can no longer pause to wonder and stand rapt in awe is as good as dead; his eyes are closed."[307] When we behold him, we exchange the dull gray of a begrudging hamster wheel existence for a full-color, hope-filled expectation that somehow every day we will see God's handiwork and supernatural displays or at least his fingerprints, that confirm he is active and with us. In Psalm 34 we read:

> Worship in awe and wonder, all you who've been made holy! For all who fear him will feast with plenty.
> Even the strong and the wealthy grow weak and hungry,
> but those who passionately pursue the Lord
> will never lack any good thing. [308]

British Bible teacher A. W. Pink stated, "Happy the soul that has been awed by a view of God's majesty."[309] This place of awe and wonder fills us with a feast of plenty. It also provides a dose of courage; the very courage we need

---

[307] Albert Einstein, *Einstein on Politics: His Private Thoughts and Public Stands on Nationalism, Zionism, War, Peace, and the Bomb*, (Princeton University Press, 2007), 229.

[308] Psalm 34:9-10, TPT

[309] A.W. Pink, *The Sovereignty of God*, (Watchmaker Publishing, 2011), 202.

to "trust our unknown future" in the hands of the "known God" who we behold each and everyday.[310]

Make it personal

1. What do you do when you read something in the Bible you do not understand?

2. Is it difficult for you to make sense of or believe in unseen realities? How do unseen realities affect your everyday experience?

3. In what ways can you creatively honor God with the talents he has given you?

4. Is there a place you have stood in nature or a work of art you have observed that pointed you heavenward? If more than one, which ones?

[310] From a quote commonly used by Corrie Ten Boom during her sermons.

Embracing Exponential

12. Our Ultimate Goal

WHEN YOU LOOK at the Westminster Shorter Catechism, the first in a long list of questions is, "What is the chief end of man?" Catechumens are taught to respond, "Man's chief end is to glorify God and enjoy him forever." In fully pursuing the exponential life promised by Jesus, we do just that. In so doing we, by default, become "glorifiers" and "enjoyers"[311] of God.

Try to imagine the greatest way to glorify God. It is to completely surrender our will and our actions, to take on the yoke of Jesus. It is to learn how to really live. When we live an exponential life, we allow his kingdom to be fully embodied in our lives. We become fully his and he becomes fully ours. As so beautifully stated by Solomon in the Song of Songs 6:3,[312] "I am my beloved's, and my beloved is mine."

We become even greater glorifiers when we who are of the "now" kingdom allow our exponential lives to serve as invading armies into the "not yet" kingdom. Paul states in 2 Corinthians 3:17-18:

---

[311] D.P. Hollinger, *To Glorify or Enjoy Forever? Knowing & Doing*, (2003), 1.

[312] KJV

> Now the Lord is the Spirit; and where the Spirit of the Lord *is*, there *is* liberty. But we all, with unveiled faces, beholding as in a mirror the glory of the Lord, are being transformed into the same image from glory to glory, just as by the Spirit of the Lord.

I see "being transformed into" the image of Jesus as living the exponential life. It is a cleaning process for the mirror of my life which is my primary method of reflecting the glory of the Lord to others — especially to those who live in darkness and are in dire need of light. If we refuse Jesus' invitation to live this full, abundant, exponential life, can we really consider ourselves enjoyers of him if we never fully embrace his gift?

It reminds me of a gift my wife and I gave to my parents. It was a DVD player that would magically erase vulgar words from movies and somehow replace them with more acceptable words. We bought it on a short trip to the States from the mission field where we serve. We wrapped it and gave it to them. They were ecstatic, but due to our tight schedule, we did not have time to hook it up. Each week I called and asked, "How are you enjoying that DVD player? And each week they collectively replied, "It's great!" After a few months, the conversation changed and I no longer asked them about it. About two years later, we had the opportunity of another visit, during which I was surprised to find they still had never even taken the DVD player out of the box! They didn't understand how to hook it up with all their existing power cords and cables. Subsequently, they just left it, unopened.

I know they were grateful, yet the reality of the situation was a bit frustrating to me as the one who had given them the gift. Without a doubt they were thankful for the gift, just as we are with our free gift of salvation, yet they were not fully enjoying it. It somewhat spoiled the joy of the effort.

That must be the way that God feels when he sees us never take his promise "out of the box" and fully enjoy it. "Eternal life is not a peculiar feeling inside! It is not your ultimate destination, to which you will go when you are dead. If you are born again, eternal life is the quality of life that you possess right now."[313] His offer to us is less about a destination and more about spending time in the journey with the one who teaches us how to truly live. Psalm 37:4 reminds us to "delight yourself in the Lord, and he will give you the desires of your heart." In this place of perfect enjoyment we find what we are really looking for in life. Augustine defined it as the God-shaped hole that made our hearts restless until they rest in him. It's that hole in your restless heart that is being filled.

Now compare my story of the unopened gift with the pure bliss that a child has toward a timely gift. The bicycle is opened and immediately taken for a spin, the ball is

---

[313] *W. Ian Thomas (1988). "The Saving Life of Christ and the Mystery of Godliness," p.140, Harper Collins*

kicked or bounced even before reaching the outdoors, and the video game is plugged in and played without hesitation. Oswald Chambers reminded us that those who become "enjoyers" will stop worrying about "messing up," "being inadequate," or "not measuring up" because they will be too busy just fully living life:

> The continual grubbing on the inside to see whether we are what we ought to be generates a self-centered, morbid type of Christianity, not the robust, simple life of the child of God... what a splendid audacity a child has, and that is what our Lord taught us to have.[314]

Just as a child has no thought of getting her clothes wet when there is a creek at hand, the deeper we wade into the waters of the exponential life, our worries diminish. In that state of splendid audacity, we lose our false selves and find our truest selves.

This truth is fully revealed when Jesus stated, "Truly I tell you, unless you change and become like little children, you will never enter the kingdom of heaven. Therefore, whoever takes the lowly position of this child is the greatest in the kingdom of heaven."[315] From this place of childlike humility and simplicity that we step into the kingdom of

---

[314] Oswald Chambers, *The Complete Works of Oswald Chambers*, (Discovery House Publishers, 2000), 239.

[315] Matthew 18:3-5, NIV

heaven. When we live an exponential life, we find that we are more concerned with missing out on what the full promise has to offer us instead of how we are somehow screwing it all up by scratching our bicycle. The glory of God is the human being fully alive. That childlike enjoyment of life is who we are when we are really alive.

Where do we go from here?

BY NOW I HOPE you know that we are not aiming for a physical destination or some high-pitched conclusion in our journey. Taking the on-ramps of these paradoxical imperatives moves us beyond mechanical motions. Over time we find that we slide into a process of becoming something more. Things begin to shift and change incrementally. We realize that we have entered the process of becoming, in which we truly glorify God. We learn to really live in each moment we have been given. As Dallas Willard put it, "As a learning process, discipleship means living interactively with his resurrected presence (through his Word, his personal presence, and through other people) as we progressively learn to lead our lives as he would if he were we."[316] It is simply the process of becoming like Jesus.

---

[316] Dallas Willard, *The Great Omission: Reclaiming Jesus's Essential Teachings on Discipleship*, (HarperOne, 2014) 166.

Some may still hold to the misconception that we are not one of those chosen to live this promised life. Those should observe the words of Symeon the New Theologian:

> And why do you pick out for yourselves the obscure passages of inspired Scripture and then tear them out of context and twist them in order to accomplish your own destruction? Do you not hear the Savior crying out every day: "As I live I have no pleasure in the death of the wicked, but that the wicked turn from his way and live" (Ezekiel 33:11)? Do you not hear Him Who says: "Repent, for the Kingdom of Heaven is at hand" (Matthew 3:2); and again: "Just so, I tell you, there is joy in heaven over one sinner who repents"? (Luke 15:7, adapted) Did He ever say to some: "Do not repent for I will not accept you," while to others who were predestined: "But you, repent! because I knew you beforehand"? Of course not! Instead, throughout the world and in every church He shouts: "Come to Me, all who labor and are heavy laden, and I will give you rest" (Matthew 11:28). Come, He says, all you who are burdened with many sins, to the One Who takes away the sin of the world; come all who thirst to the fountain which flows and never dies.[317]

[317] Symeon the New Theologian, *On the Mystical Life: Second Ethical Discourse*, (Saint Vladimir's Press, 1996), Commentary on Matthew 3:2.

When he says *all,* that includes you, this invitation is often ignored or overlooked.

We focus on the urgent or the shiny new things our society offers, all while turning a blind eye to the reality that Gregory the Dialogist pointed out:

> "The kingdom of heaven is at hand." Even if the gospel were to be silent, dearly beloved, the world now proclaims this message. Its ruins are its words. Struck by so many blows, it has fallen from its glory. It is as if the world itself reveals to us now that another kingdom is near, which will succeed it. It is abhorred by the very people who loved it. Its own ruins preach that it should not be loved. If someone's house were shaken and threatened with ruin, whoever lived in it would flee. The one who loved it when it was standing would hasten to leave it as soon as possible when it was falling. Therefore if the world is falling, and we embrace it by loving it, we are choosing rather to be overwhelmed than to live in it. Nothing separates us from its ruin insofar as our love binds us by our attachment to it. It is easy now, when we see everything heading for destruction, to disengage our minds from love of the world. But then it was very difficult, because the disciples were sent to preach the unseen kingdom of heaven at the very time when

> everyone far and wide could see the kingdoms of earth flourishing.[318]

Think as well of Jesus' tears in Luke 19:42, 44, when he exclaimed, "Oh, that you would know the things that made for peace...because you did not know the time of your visitation."[319] That ellipsis is for you just as much as it was for Jerusalem. It is one of history's most pregnant pauses. Oh, that you would have taken up his invitation to live an exponential life. He weeps at your missed opportunity.

No failure in falling, only in not trying

OTHERS MAKE NO ATTEMPT because they fear that somehow they may fail. In my pursuit of this promised life, I have come to realize that the only way to fail is simply not to trust in God's unlimited power and his promise to me concerning the exponential life, to not follow his on-ramps that lead me to the thin places in my soul. You will fail in some way or another in your attempt to learn from Jesus, but take heart; you are on a well-worn path taken by generations and generations of men and women who have walked into the exponential life.

---

[318] Manlio Simonetti, *Ancient Christian Commentary on Scripture: Matthew 1-13*, (InterVarsity Press, 2014), commentary on Matthew 10:7.
[319] ESV

These imperatives we learn by practice, the same way you learned to ride a bicycle. Books, like this one, are designed to inspire, guide, and give direction. But no one ever learned to ride a bike by reading a book about it. We are not born listeners nor radically generous. We must learn to be if we want to reach the thin places of our soul and as a result live an exponential life.

I can take you to the hill where I learned to ride a bike and I can take you to the little country church and stand at the spot where I learned to pray. It wasn't in a singular attempt in either case, but it involved a vision, an intention, and a means. We strive, as Jesus commanded us to in Luke 13:24, but we never stress. But how? Simply by remembering that we are not attempting to earn anything from God, but rather we are striving to live the life we were created to live.

Those opening days of Bike Riding 101 were just as painful as they were glorious. Thomas Aquinas said, "Slothful persons always allege obstacles as an excuse."[320] There seemed to always be an obstacle waiting to be transformed into an excuse for quitting. The bike was a girl's bike. What if my friends saw me? The chain would slip. What if I flipped over the handlebars?

But I was undeterred. There was a lot of falling involved, several failed attempts, and a lot of tears and frus-

[320] Thomas Aquinas from his commentary on Hebrews 6:3 found in the *Patristic Bible Commentary: Commentary on the Epistle of Hebrews*, 309.

tration, but I was determined to keep getting back on until it became second nature. This trap of turning obstacles into excuses has been true each time I endeavored to take a new on-ramp.

Even when you fall, don't stop. Keep pressing. Get back up and see where it leads you. The journey may not go exactly where you wanted to go, but many times it will lead where you never knew you really wanted or needed to go. I call this spiritual serendipity. In the kingdom of God, I have yet to find an on-ramp that leads to nowhere. They all eventually lead us somewhere. We must trust the on-ramps Jesus left us and, in our obedience, be amazed by where he really wanted to take us in the first place. As motivational speaker Zig Ziglar found out, "Difficult roads often lead to beautiful destinations."[321] Ask yourself, where does God want to take me? Am I willing to go there?

These on-ramps may not lead us as far as we may have hoped, or where we thought we would be going, but they must be seen as a means of opening us up to God. These paradoxical imperatives allow the Father, Son, and Holy Spirit to establish a beachhead on the shores of our life that we have yet to fully yield to Him. When we do, the enemy loses ground and little by little we turn ourselves over to our Lord.

---

[321] Quote commonly used in talks by speaker Zig Ziglar

Write yourself a letter

THESE ON-RAMPS do not just lead us into a swamp of nowhere. We are like the maple trees around my childhood house. I remember my older brother jumping over them in a tumbling act for our family. He never lacked for energy. They grew in plain sight, but went largely unnoticed by those of us who walked past them each day. It wasn't until I was a teenager and received a letter from home while away at Bible college that I noticed their drastic change. They included a photo in the envelope which featured the trees in the background. They were enormous and reached twice as high as our roof. They had soared over time and were no longer little in size. Spiritually, we are like those trees. No one ever really watches a tree grow.

My wife and I have a custom of mailing ourselves a postcard from the places we travel. Usually it's one with a nice photo of something we saw that we don't want to forget. A castle, a beach, a vista or a sunset are the normal offerings we have found. We write only a few lines of what we have been able to explore and we mail it. The older I get, the more I enjoy looking over the scrapbook that is filled with them. There are dozens from countless day trips, weeklong vacations, work trips, and holiday getaways. As soon as I see them, it jars my long term memory enough to take me back to each place and remember the sights and sounds. None of them were useless trips, because of the memories made and treasured. We must chart our spiritual growth and journal to remind ourselves where we have been in our journey.

One of the best things I have found is to write an honest letter to God about my real struggles and challenges. I include hopeful expectations, the areas I want to grow in, and the things I want to see transformed in my life. Then, I seal it up and don't read it for a few years. Like the effect of the photos and postcards, I find that I am more likely to see some growth, even maturity, that completely surprises me. You will smile when you recall the places you have been spiritually on this journey toward your full exponential.

Pace yourself for the long haul

WE ARE NOT patient creatures. This is confirmed by our penchant for fast food, fast travel, fast fixes, and fast answers. "We are too often double espresso followers of a decaf Sovereign."[322] Dallas Willard told John Ortberg the one thing he needed to take on his new season in life that would bring ever-increasing demands on him was to "ruthlessly eliminate hurry."[323] He was firing a shot at the mon-

---

[322] John Ortberg, *If You Want to Walk on Water, You've Got to Get Out of the Boat*, (Zondervan, 2014), 250.

[323] John Ortberg, *Soul Keeping: Caring for the Most Important Part of You*, (Zondervan, 2014), 22.

ster that sinks the greatest number of ships among those that are sailing toward the exponential life. This journey that Jesus has invited us to take is on his time, not ours. This flies in the face of our deep-seated illusion of time.

What God desires and needs from us does not include hurry. Instead, he asks for patience for the slowness of the work that is taking place in our lives. As Russian writer Leo Tolstoy said, "Patience is waiting. Not passively waiting. That is laziness. But to keep going when the going is hard and slow — that is patience. The two most powerful warriors are patience and time."[324] This commitment to wait on the process while continuing to press in is vital.

The famous verse of Isaiah 40:31 reminds us, "But they that wait upon the Lord shall renew their strength; they shall mount up with wings as eagles; they shall run, and not be weary; and they shall walk, and not faint."[325] David Hubbard analyzed this, noting that those who wait patiently on the Lord and continue pressing in their commitment will fly, run, and walk. There are times we will fly and reach unexpected heights in our journey. Other times, he reminds us that we will only reach a brisk run and not grow weary. In these grounded times, don't grow weary. "Your time will come. Just keep running." Then, too, are seasons

---

[324] This quote is commonly attributed to Russian author Leo Tolstoy, but some think it may have possibly been coined earlier by Augustine of Hippo.

[325] KJV

when all you can muster will be a walk, but keep moving forward in your commitment. "Sometimes walking is all you can do. But in those times, walking is enough."[326]

Over the course of my journey toward the exponential life, it has become clear that intentionality plus frequency produces desired results. Our results have nothing to do with earning, but they will by nature produce an increased impulse toward obedient effort. As Scottish theologian Peter T. Forsythe explained, "The first duty of every soul is to find not its freedom but its Master."[327] Ultimately this impulse toward obedience is about the determination and effort to simply keep moving forward. However, in the current state of the church, it seems these two basic qualities are rare.

A. W. Tozer reminds us that this is nothing new. He saw this lack of effort in the past millennium.

> The amount of loafing practiced by the average Christian in spiritual things would ruin a concert pianist if he allowed himself to do the same thing in the field of music. The idle puttering around that we see in church circles would end the career of a big league pitcher in one week. No scientist could solve his exacting problem

---

[326] John Ortberg, *If You Want to Walk on Water, You've Got to Get Out of the Boat*, (Zondervan, 2014), 269.

[327] Charles Swindoll, *Joseph: A Man of Integrity and Forgiveness*, (Thomas Nelson, 1998), 181.

> if he took as little interest in it as the rank and file of Christians take in the art of being holy. The nation whose soldiers were as soft and undisciplined as the soldiers of the churches would be conquered by the first enemy that attacked it. Triumphs are not won by men in easy chairs. Success is costly.[328]

The exponential life is not found in magic mantras or heavy-handed compliance. It appears when a disciple is willingly determined to keep moving in the quest of obedient effort, regardless of the personal cost.

Planning your pursuit of the exponential life

WHAT WOULD YOUR REACTION be if, in the middle of a casual conversation, I asked you to pray for me, specifically about trying to earn a spot on the Olympic figure skating team? You would most likely ask in amazement, "I never knew you could skate competitively." I would respond, "I don't skate at all, but I am passionate about trying."

As a middle-aged, moderately out of shape, uncoordinated man, you would comment about the absurdity of the

[328] A.W. Tozer, *We Travel an Appointed Way*, (Christian Publications, 1988), 26-27.

petition, or at least advise me to forget it, lest I hurt myself. No one ever becomes a successful businessperson, world-class athlete, top chef, or an accomplished musician by simply trying. It only comes as the result of training.

Nor should you think that you will become a true disciple of Jesus, an image bearer living an exponential life, without doing the same. My missionary friend Sonia Crawley teaches up and coming missionaries that, "Training is always better than trying." The apostle Peter admonished Christ followers[329] when he pointed to Jesus as the example whose steps they should follow. Theologian T.B. Maston taught his seminary students that "All the claims of Christ can be summed up in two words — 'Follow Me'."[330] The exponential life will be found by disciples who develop a spiritual training plan based on effort, as opposed to earning.

Training of any type, whether physical or spiritual, is best done with a plan. Your plan should include a schedule that focuses on implementing the on-ramps into your daily, weekly, monthly and yearly rhythms. Daily times are deliberate and frequent for listening to God's voice in the written Word. Fixed multiple opportunities take precedence each day to refocus and reform your life through arranged asking

---

[329] 1 Peter 2:21b

[330] From a sermon written by Rick Lance, https://www.preaching.com/sermons/discipleship-following-in-his-footsteps/

through prayer, mixed with intentional walks into wilderness as well as an unwavering commitment to your faith community.

It should include a pledge to practice a radical form of generosity with money, mercy, finances, and forgiveness, as well as the vow to see Sabbath as integral to your overall well-being and to your exponential life. Self-denial, as John the Baptist saw, is central in our plan: "I must decrease, that he might increase." Each time you say no to self through fasting or abstinence, you are giving space for grace to fill your life. And finally the promise to walk slowly through moments that are ripe for beholding, through creation, through art, through music, and through other image bearers.

These on-ramps should never be viewed as obligations, but rather as opportunities, opportunities that open us up to the grace of God in our heart, soul, mind, and strength. Opportunities that require frequency and intentionality to cultivate the exponential life Jesus has invited us to live. What would your life look like if you spent as much effort in obedience, in training as a disciple, in following the on-ramps that Jesus taught and modeled as you do in cleaning up the consequences of doing life your way?

Even with a plan that brings rhythms into our daily life, the growth we will see at times can be slower than we like. I have found great inspiration in the words French theologian Pierre Teilhard de Chardin wrote of the process:

Above all, trust in the slow work of God.
We are quite naturally impatient in everything to reach the end without delay.
We should like to skip the intermediate stages.
We are impatient of being on the way to something unknown, something new.
And yet it is the law of all progress
that it is made by passing through some stages of instability —
and that it may take a very long time.
And so I think it is with you;
your ideas mature gradually — let them grow,
let them shape themselves, without undue haste.
Don't try to force them on,
as though you could be today what time
(that is to say, grace and circumstances acting on your own good will)
will make of you tomorrow.
Only God could say what this new spirit
gradually forming within you will be.
Give Our Lord the benefit of believing
that his hand is leading you,
and accept the anxiety of feeling yourself
in suspense and incomplete.[331]

---

331 Hearts on Fire; Praying with the Jesuits, (Loyola Press, 2005), 102.

Trust God is working, even if it seems like he is working slowly. Determine to get back in the saddle every time you fall, no matter how many times that might be, and choose to enjoy the process. As 19th century English minister James Sherman reminds us, "You can't go back and make a new start, but you can start right now and make a brand new ending."[332] The exponential life is a gift, not a penitence. It will lead you to finally becoming the exponential person God created you to be.

[332] James Sherman, *Rejection*, (Pathway Books, 1982), 45.

Conclusion

TO LAND THIS PLANE on which we have been traveling, I circle back to conclude where we began, in a comment gently nestled inside the corner of a casual conversation, but a different comment and another conversation. A missionary colleague inadvertently helped to keep me on track in my pursuit for the exponential life. I heard what would forever change my life slide nonchalantly from Rocky's conversation.

We expounded on the challenges presented in the lives of missionaries, like where would the financial backing come from for the projects we had in mind? Or what were we to do to overcome the seemingly perpetual conflict from national church leaders and even between other missionaries? As a result, he confessed that he had learned to live under only one question, and it had made all the difference. He simply asked himself at the end of each day, "Was Jesus happy?"

He learned to strive toward an affirmative answer to that question and everything else seemed to fall into place. He expressed a commonly held age-old truth that has been passed down among the true disciples of Jesus over the past two millennia. Yoking yourself to Jesus has never been easy, nor has it ever been complicated.

Perhaps more to the point was the understanding that Saint Patrick had of the true goal of the exponential life. During his ministry he took Psalm 46:10 and composed this meditation.

> Be still and know that I am God.
> Be still and know that I am.
> Be still and know.
> Be still.
> Be.[333]

It is so simple and so uncomplicated. We only need to trust and follow Jesus and become our true selves that he created us to be and to live each day of our lives to answer affirmatively but one question: "Was Jesus happy?" One final word of advice: never overlook the power of a comment gently nestled inside the corner of a casual conversation.

---

[333] This prayer is commonly attributed to the Irish saint and is found in the work of Charles H. H. Wright, *The Writings of St. Patrick: The Apostle of Ireland; A Revised Translation with Notes Critical and Historical*, 3rd ed., Christian Classic Series 6 (Woking and London: Religious Tract Society, 1878).

Make it personal

1. Which on-ramp do you expect will be the most challenging to implement into your life?

2. Which on-ramps are you currently experiencing success in pursuing?

3. How do you respond to failure when it occurs in your life?

4. Write a letter today to commemorate where you are. Choose a time in the near future to check back in and write a new one.

More from the Author

Join us as we reach back, lean in, and seek out a deeper experience with God. Go deeper with host Joil Marbut at *Sage Spirituality* Podcast on all listening platforms and sagespirituality.com.

SAGE Spirituality

JOIL A MARBUT

Find more titles and upcoming releases at fscpublishing.com

Made in the USA
Columbia, SC
09 April 2024